money makeover

The **secret** to **budgeting, saving** and **investing** for **financial success**

Nina Dubecki
Vanessa Rowsthorn

moneygirl.com.au

First published 2010 by Wrightbooks
an imprint of John Wiley & Sons Australia, Ltd
42 McDougall Street, Milton Qld 4064

Office also in Melbourne

Typeset in Giovanni Book 10.5/13

© Nina Dubecki and Vanessa Rowsthorn 2010

The moral rights of the authors have been asserted

National Library of Australia Cataloguing-in-Publication data:

Author:	Dubecki, Nina.
Title:	Money makeover: the secret to budgeting, saving and investing for financial success/Nina Dubecki, Vanessa Rowsthorn.
ISBN:	9781742469577 (pbk.)
Notes:	Includes index.
Subjects:	Budgets, personal. Finance, personal. Saving and investment.
Other Authors/ Contributors:	Rowsthorn, Vanessa.
Dewey Number:	649.122

Cover design by Brad Maxwell

Author image: Lydia Baic

Cover image © iStockphoto.com/Nathalie Beauvois

Printed in Australia by McPherson's Printing Group

10 9 8 7 6 5 4 3 2 1

contents

acknowledgements

We'd like to raise a glass to the inspirational women of MALICE, Nick Davies (website whiz), Lydia Baic (Moneygirl design guru), Jason Eveleigh (bean counter extraordinaire) and Jason Mullen (research ace).

A huge thank you to the team at Wiley and to all of the women who've shared their stories with us. And last, but certainly not least, we thank our families and friends for their ongoing support and for putting up with us. You're the best.

introduction

It's not you, it's me ... or is it?

Let's not beat around the bush: finance can be dull. Not mildly dull, but eye-glazingly, sleep-inducingly dull. If you're looking in from the outside, the world of finance is an intimidating planet inhabited by grey-suited men; the finance segment of the news is spoken like it's in another language; and the investment pages of the paper seem to hold little more relevance to the modern woman than tomorrow's weather report for Vladivostok.

It's easy to feel overwhelmed — stupid, even. But the simple fact is that not many people do understand all the intricacies of financial investment — even those who work in the field (though they'd never admit it — hello, GFC). You're not dumb; it's just that you're not being communicated to in a way that's relevant to you.

It's also easy to avoid thinking about your own financial future. There's nothing appealing about trying to picture yourself 30 years from now. It's bad enough thinking about what you'll look like (yikes), let alone thinking about being poor as well. It's so much easier to live for now and spend what you want, when you want, leaving the rest to worry about later.

But what if — just what if — you had the chance to change your life *Sliding Doors* style? What if doing a bit of work now meant you could ultimately live the life of your choice, whatever that meant to you? You might have dreams of travelling the world, becoming a property or sharemarket mogul, giving all your money away to worthy causes, or even spending your days wearing a sequinned miniskirt and splashing your cash on the Gold Coast. (Hey, we won't judge you.) It's all about having the freedom to choose.

The truth is that it's not actually that hard to get smart with money and to learn how to invest — you just have to know where to start and have a desire to learn.

I say tomayto, you say tomarto

You might be asking yourself why we'd write a book just for women. Well, as women, we face distinct challenges and tend to approach money and investment quite differently to men. This is in part because the financial independence of women is a relatively recent phenomenon, and it's brought about a gamut of issues that could earn a shrink a fortune.

Etched into the female psyche are centuries of not needing to earn an income for ourselves. Even if we don't like to admit it, sometimes we wait before taking control of our finances: we wait until we meet our soul mate before we think about buying a house; or we cross our fingers that our future partner will earn a mint. Sometimes when we're partnered up we find it easier to leave investing to our other half. We might not want to appear to be interfering in financial matters or we may feel stupid asking too many questions. And sometimes, quite frankly, we're just not all that interested. Our lives are so busy that it's easier to leave investing our money to someone else.

However, there are some very sobering statistics that show just why it's so important that women get smart with their money — preferably earlier rather than later. On average, women live longer than men. Women earn less than their male counterparts, and are more likely to take time out of the workplace. All this adds up to a future where as a woman you're likely to have far less money up your sleeve than men — yet it's meant to stretch far longer.

Since we started our website <www.moneygirl.com.au>, we've been surprised to discover that most of the emails we receive are not from young women wanting to know where to start. They're primarily from 45- to 55-year-old women who, for various reasons, have very little money put away and aren't sure what to do. So it was no real surprise when we started researching for this book to discover that in 2009, women aged between 55 and 64 only had average savings of $60 700 to support themselves for the rest of their lives. Now that's a scary statistic.

Without starting to burn our bras, we do want to stress how important it is for women to take control of their own financial futures. If Prince Charming turns up, that's fantastic. But if he doesn't (or if he turns out to be slightly less charming than anticipated) then at least you'll have given yourself the best chance of getting set up on your own.

Anything you can do, I can do better

After all this talk of doom and gloom, it's time for some good news: women are biologically geared to be much better investors than men. We may never beat a man in the 100 metre sprint, but give us the stock exchange as a playing field and we can more than give him a run for his money.

There have been many studies over the past 20 years that concur in their findings that women are the fairer sex when it comes to returns on the sharemarket. In 2004, a British study of 100 000 share portfolios found that on average, women's portfolios grew by more than 10 per cent that year, while men's only grew by 6 per cent over the same time frame.

Another ground-breaking study, carried out by Merrill Lynch Investment Management in 2005, examined the investment mistakes of 1000 American investors and the attitudes and beliefs related to those mistakes. They found conclusively that women make fewer investment mistakes than men, and make them less often. Reasons cited for these results related to our natural psychological make-up: women tend be less confident than men when it comes to investing, and so are more likely to research, to ask questions and to seek expert advice. We are also more likely than men to stick to a plan, and are less likely to try to 'time the market' or trade too often.

So it seems that women are well equipped with all the right tools for financial success — it's just a question of having the know-how and confidence to use them.

Money makeover

So, how should you go about attaining the money smarts and confidence you need to become financially independent? Well, if we may have a moment of cheeky self-promotion, by reading this book, you're already off to a mighty good start. But let's start with what this book will *not* do:

$ It won't speak to you as if you're obsessed with shoes, shopping or sales.

$ It won't tell you how to get rich overnight — although we will show you to how to build your fortune in a slower, surer way.

$ It won't man-bash. Quite frankly, we think men are pretty neat. We just want you to give them a red-hot run for their money in the investment stakes.

Instead, this book is designed to be practical. We've read mountains of finance books and found that all too often we finish these books feeling inspired, but with no idea where to begin or how to apply the information to our own situations. So when we wrote this book, we wanted to make sure that every topic was covered in a logical order. This way, you'll be able to work your way through the book and sort out your finances step by step. Plus, we've always tried to show you exactly *how* to go about implementing any investments you are keen on — such as buying shares or property.

We've also written the book with you in mind. We don't expect you to have a degree in economics or to earn megabucks. We've done our darnedest to make the content interesting and relevant, breaking down financial lingo and using as many real-life examples as possible. The book is jam-packed with stories of how real women have invested their money and what they've learned along the way. We've even included a little limerick at the start of each chapter — now, what other finance book out there has *ditties*, we ask you?

Finally, we wanted our book to be comprehensive. This isn't just a book on budgeting; it covers everything from saving to investing to all of those extra things you need to know about, such as insurance and even how to deal with money when you're in a relationship.

In order to walk you step by step through your money makeover, we've divided the book up into four sections:

§ *Part I* is all about getting yourself sorted out before you become an investor — understanding your goals, working your way out of debt, learning great saving strategies and getting a grip on the basic concepts and terminology you'll need to understand as you move forward. You can't be a successful investor and achieve financial success until you have the basics down pat.

§ *Part II* is where we ramp things up a notch and cover the four major types of investment: shares, managed funds, superannuation and property. While you might not think every type of investment is your cup of tea, we urge you to read about them all anyway. You never know which one is going to tickle your fancy, and it'll help you to make an educated decision about what's best for you.

§ *Part III* deals with all the extra things you need to consider as a part of your financial plan. We'll show you how you can invest without feeling like you're selling your soul, how to insure yourself properly and how you can factor in life's little curve balls (like heading overseas to work, shacking up with your significant other or having a little bambino).

$\mathcal{S}$ *Part IV* reveals the secret to financial success. You'll find out what sets apart those people who become financially independent and those who get lost along the way. We've read, researched and pondered this deeply over a vino or two, and we're pretty sure we know the secret to financial success and how you can make it work for you.

We're well aware that in finance land, some topics are way, *way* less exciting than others — reading about insurance, for example, is unlikely to ever set your pulse racing in eager anticipation. But we can't stress enough how important it is not to skip past these less-enticing sections. Think of it like eating All-Bran: it's dry, but you know a small dose will help you avoid a — er — tight bind later.

We hope that by the time you reach the end of this book you'll be set on a path to financial freedom that will liberate you in the most fabulous way.

And so begins your money makeover.

Our story

Like Thelma and Louise, but without the cliff-top ending (or, sadly, Brad Pitt), our story begins with a road trip: two colleagues en route to a funeral in rural Victoria. Sitting in a car together dressed in black, we nattered away for hours — until somehow the conversation turned to investing, and the lack of interesting information out there for women like us. So we made a decision then and there to start a money club, where we'd meet up with our female friends once a month to talk finance. We figured a good gasbag and drink at a bar would be as good an incentive as any to learn more about investing, and so MALICE (Most Ace Ladies' Investment Club of Excellence) was born. Before we knew it, it was a year later and we had all made significant steps forward — properties were purchased, super was sorted, shares were bought. In one way or another, the club changed all of our lives.

During this time we were madly in pursuit of learning. We read anything financial we could get our mitts on, from websites to books and magazines, even delving into the scary depths of talkback radio. What we discovered was jargon-filled, overwhelming and desperately dull. We realised there was a real need for female-friendly finance information, so we decided to take the money club idea one step further and create a website where women could go online to share their experiences and learn more. Although we were both working full-time, we met every Sunday for two years to work on the website. We coerced talented friends into helping us with our website and spent a good chunk of our lives tracking down the best financial resources we could. Finally, in July 2009, <www.moneygirl.com.au> went live — and the response has been fantastic.

We are not financial advisers. In fact, neither of us have financial backgrounds at all. But we have something we think is far more valuable: an understanding of what it's like to be a woman earning an average wage and who is a successful investor on the road to financial independence. This book is the culmination of everything we have learnt along the way.

Nina and Vanessa

Become a Moneygirl

Moneygirl.com.au is our online home. It's a website with links to all the best bits of other finance sites. It features regularly updated finance news plus forums where you can talk to like-minded women. You'll also find one-click links to all of the websites mentioned in this book.

part I
getting it together

So here's where your money makeover starts.

Before you do anything else, you'll need to get your current financial situation sorted out — you can't become a successful investor until you have a true picture of where you stand financially and a good understanding of where you want to go.

In part I, we'll cover everything you'll need to know in order to put yourself in the best position possible to start investing. And while things like setting goals and putting together a savings plan can sound all too much like hard work, you should never underestimate how important they are in swinging financial fortune in your favour.

In the next four chapters you will:

$ work out what money means to you

$ learn about good and bad debt (and how to get rid of the bad)

$ pick up some budgeting tips

$ uncover a couple of nifty techniques to help you save more than you ever thought possible

$ learn the fundamentals of becoming an investor.

Go forth and conquer!

chapter 1

setting your goals

There once was a girl called Sheree
Who dreamt of sailing the sea
She wrote a great plan
Worked hard as one can
And now sails her yacht off Fiji.

Ah, money. We have such a complex relationship with it. On the one hand we've grown up being taught that 'money makes the world go round'; and yet on the other hand, we're taught that 'money isn't everything'. Confused, anyone?

Before you can jump on the path to financial success, you need to look at the way you think about money and get rid of any preconceived ideas and bad money habits that might be holding you back. Like it or not, money affects every aspect of your life from where you live to how you live, so it's vital that you're the one calling the shots in your relationship, not the other way around.

You also need to stop for a moment and decide on your financial goals. Life whizzes by so fast that if you don't pause to give serious thought as to what you want to achieve financially (and why), future decisions may get made on the run without taking into account what's really important to you.

Then, as with any good makeover, you need to commit yourself to taking action. As they say, there's no time like the present—so giddy-up! In this chapter we'll cover:

§ your relationship with money: taking a look at yourself in the mirror

§ money myths: 10 thoughts to banish forever

§ setting goals: working out what you want to achieve

§ taking ownership: committing to making it happen.

Your relationship with money: taking a look at yourself in the mirror

As trusty old Dr Phil will tell you, you can't move forward until you have addressed the past. The same goes for your relationship with money. Over the years you've probably collected baggage that you might not even know you have.

Often the way people behave with money is not built on reason, but on emotion. For example, splashing out on an expensive dress can be more about getting swept up in the adrenaline of a shopper's high (or perhaps caught in the grips of a very persuasive salesperson) than anything else. How you think about money can also be related to what you've been taught (or not been taught) growing up. Your family's attitude towards money can have a huge influence on the way you behave. If you grew up hearing that the only chance you'll ever have of becoming wealthy is by making it as a high-flying lawyer or a doctor, why would you think otherwise?

Nina's story (age 39)

It was completely by accident that I became interested in investing. In fact, until my mid-20s I'd thought my only chance of becoming wealthy would be to marry someone rich or to win Tattslotto. These were notions my parents had unconsciously instilled in me, but not through any fault of their own — it's just that no-one had ever taught them about money, either.

About 12 years ago, I was in the city one Saturday afternoon when it started to rain, so I ran into a bookshop to escape. Walking down the aisles a book called *The Wealthy Barber* caught my eye and I picked it up and started to flick through. I'd never read a book about money before, but this one sounded interesting and seemed accessible so I paid for it and left. Reading it later that night was a revelation. For the first time in my life, I realised that I wouldn't ever have to worry about money again if I took a few simple steps. I understood that my financial future was firmly in my hands.

Luckily, I didn't have any credit card debt — that was one thing my parents had taught me about money: to always pay my credit card balance off in full every month. So the first thing I did was to open a managed fund with $2000, after which I committed to monthly direct debits of $200 straight out of my bank account. In the space of three years, the balance had grown to around $20 000. I'd also saved enough for a deposit on a little apartment in the inner city. It was the start of my life as an investor.

It's time to air your dirty laundry

Do you have any long-held notions about money that aren't doing you any favours? Have a good think about your attitude towards money. For example, do you think you're just not one of 'the lucky ones' and that you'll never be well off? Or are you waiting for that big pay rise or Tattslotto windfall to head your way before you start investing? Consider the way you behave with money and look at your habits closely — try to be as honest as you can. By understanding your attitude towards money and committing to changing those beliefs and behaviours you're taking your first step towards financial success.

Examples of bad habits

Just like biting your nails, there are plenty of bad money habits that hold women back when it comes to taking control of their finances. Do any of these sound a little too familiar?

$ *Pay Cheque Patty* lives from pay cheque to pay cheque, finding herself with no savings and no cash left over at the end of each month.

$ *Spendy Sasha* finds it hard to resist a sale and easily gets caught up in buying frenzies, purchasing things she doesn't really need, only to regret it later.

$ *Generous Georgie* shouts dinner and drinks for her partner, friends and family way too frequently. She spends too much on gifts, and often finds that she doesn't have enough money to pay for essential living costs and bills for herself later. Generous Georgie has been spotted 'loaning' money to family members and friends who she knows are unlikely to pay it back.

$ *No-Responsibility Nicki* knows she's bad with money, but takes little action to change. Nicki knows that she can call on her friends, family and partner for a loan whenever she needs help — so she does.

$ *Credit-Happy Chrissie* views the money she has on her credit card as her own, and is all too happy to whip out the plastic to buy things she knows deep down she can't afford. Chrissie usually finds herself unable to pay off her credit card balance each month.

$ *Bad-Deal Belinda* doesn't shop around for a good deal on anything — bank interest rates, mobile phone deals, a new fridge, you name it. She never asks for a pay rise or promotion although she knows she deserves it.

• •

Try this

Confession time

Grab yourself a notebook. At the top of the first page write: 'Money habits I want to change'. Think of at least three things you recognise as bad money habits you want to change and jot them in your book. Writing things down can really help as it makes them 'real' and will give you a reference point to come back to later on.

• •

Money myths: 10 thoughts to banish forever

We're a nation of list lovers — rich lists, best (and worst) dressed lists, the Triple J Hottest 100 list, we love them all. So we thought we'd join the ranks of list builders and come up with our very own. Without further ado we present the 'Top 10 myths about money that you must banish from your mind' list:

1   *Money is dirty.* While accumulating riches for the sake of it or aspiring to have three sports cars sitting in your garage could be considered questionable pursuits, having money can give you the power to do good by supporting the causes you believe in. It also gives you personal freedom. There are many ways to invest your money ethically and in line with your personal beliefs. We'll talk about this in chapter 9.

2 *You can only become rich if you marry someone wealthy or win Tattslotto.* Apart from the fact that your chances of winning the lottery are pretty small, you're actually very capable of becoming independently wealthy over the long term if you acquire the right knowledge and exercise discipline. By using your money smarts you can create a comfortable future for yourself on your own terms, rather than leaving it to chance.

3 *I don't earn enough to be an investor.* Becoming a financial guru has very little to do with how much you earn. There are many examples of people on über-high salaries who squander their earnings away, and of people on average incomes who've learnt to invest wisely and become wealthy and financially free. Of course, it's easier if you're bringing home the big bucks, but it's absolutely not a prerequisite for financial success and happiness. You have to start somewhere, and as little as a few thousand dollars is enough to get you on your way.

4 *I work hard for my money and deserve to spend it on whatever I want.* Sure, you can spend your hard-earned cash on three lattes, lunch and rounds of drinks after work each day if that's what you really want. But is it really what you want to spend your money on? Or is it just habit? If you saved some of that money and invested it wisely, in a few years it could mean the difference between having enough for a deposit on your own apartment and living with your parents or renting indefinitely.

5 *Finance talk is boring and doesn't interest me enough to get my finances in order.* There's no denying that the finance news can be as effective a sleep aid as a warm glass of milk. But the truth is that you don't need to know how the All Ordinaries are performing every day in order to be successful with money. Financial success is all about knowing where to source the best, most relevant information, and getting the basics right. There are plenty

of low-maintenance investments out there, so you won't have to spend every waking hour keeping an eye on your money.

6   *I'd prefer to leave the task of managing my finances to my father/partner/accountant.* You should always be involved in any decisions made about your own finances — never hand over responsibility for your investments to someone else. While they may genuinely have your best interests at heart, you don't know how much they really know. Even if you see a financial adviser or accountant, you should always understand exactly what investments they are recommending, and know where your money is going.

7   *I'm too old now to do anything about my finances.* While getting your act into gear when you're young will certainly give you a fantastic head start, there's no such thing as being too old to get your finances sorted out. In fact, the longer you stall, the harder you'll make it for yourself in the long run.

8   *Investing is risky, so I prefer to leave my money safe and sound in a bank account.* All investment carries an element of risk, but with knowledge and research you'll learn which investment style suits you best and how you can minimise the risks. The problem with keeping money in your bank account is that it becomes victim to that nasty thing called inflation. By leaving money in a bank earning low interest over a long period of time, you'll find that your savings won't keep pace with the rising costs of living. Ironically, it can actually be one of the least-safe options over the long term. You'll read more about this in chapter 4.

9   *I'm not smart enough to invest on my own.* While finance-speak is pretty high up in the gobbledegook stakes, you don't need to have a PhD to sort out your finances. The fundamental principles of investing are actually simple, even if finance jargon is overwhelming at first. The truth is that anyone can learn to invest smartly.

Plus, super-intelligent people don't necessarily make great investors — research conducted by the US Bureau of Labor Statistics that studied 7400 people over a 30-year time span has found that there is no relationship between a person's IQ and the amount of wealth they have.

10 *I've got too much on my plate now to worry about it — I'll think about it later.* It's easy to freeze into inactivity because the idea of sorting out your finances is all too overwhelming, and it's so hard to figure out where to begin. But we can't stress how much better off you'll be if you start now. It's amazing what a difference time can make to your investments — you'll read more in chapter 3 about exactly how much better off you'll be by starting early.

If you found any of our 10 myths hitting a bit too close to home, it's time to take some positive action and banish them from your mind forever! Recognising any negative thought patterns you might have is the first step to moving forward. For example, if you're putting off making big financial decisions because you think you don't have the time, then you need to acknowledge that this is holding you back. Bite the bullet, put aside a few hours one weekend and start sorting yourself out. You'll be surprised at how quickly you can start to make proactive changes.

Setting goals: working out what you want to achieve

Once you've cast aside any barriers that might have been preventing you from getting your finances in order, it's time to work out what financial success means to you.

Money means different things to different people. Does having money mean security to you? Or is it about choice, and having the freedom to do the things you enjoy most? Whatever it is, it will be highly personal and it will probably take a little bit of consideration before you get to the bottom of it. But we urge you to take the time to think about what financial success would ultimately give you. Once you work that out, you'll have a powerful motivator to get your finances on track.

Setting your goals

Once you understand why money is important to you, you should break it down a little further. Think more specifically about what you want to achieve over different time frames. This is important, not only because it gives you objectives to aim for, but also because it will determine what sort of investment choices you make a bit later on. Importantly, aim high! Write down anything you really want, even if you have no idea yet how you might get it. The sky's the limit. Use the following time frames to work out your goals:

$ short-term (now to three years)

$ medium-term (three to five years)

$ long-term (over five years)

$ super-long-term (light years away, when you're heading out to pasture).

• •

Try this

Write down your goals

Open up a new page in your book, write the heading 'Goals' and underneath write the sub-headings 'Short-term', Medium-term', 'Long-term' and 'Super-long-term'. Beneath each of these write any specific goals that come to mind. Your goals will change over time, but this will be a great point to start from.

Here's an example of what your goals might look like:

Short-term (now to three years)

→   Pay off credit cards and personal loans.

→   Start a savings plan.

→   Take an overseas holiday.

Medium-term (three to five years)

→   Buy a car.

Long-term (five years onward)

→   Buy a house or apartment.

→   Be financially set up to start a family.

Super-long-term (light years away)

→   Retire with an annual income of $39 000 (in today's dollars).

• •

Your goals may seem a bit airy-fairy at the moment, and you're probably wondering how on earth you're going to achieve them. Don't worry about that for the time being. As you read through this book you'll learn about different investment options and money-making techniques, and in the final chapter we'll show you how to apply what you've read in the book to real life in order to help you to make your goals become reality.

Taking ownership: committing to making it happen

Women earn more money now than at any time in the past, yet studies have shown that we aren't a very confident bunch when it comes to investing. By committing yourself to learning and taking action now, you'll ensure your financial security in years to come. Here are three ways to make it happen:

1   *Make financial security a priority.* Make your money makeover a priority over the next 12 months. Work out

what financial success would ultimately mean to you and write down your goals. Make sure you keep your goals somewhere visible, and keep your money notebook close at hand so you can write things down when you need to.

2   *Open your eyes to the world of investment.* Start by reading the money supplement in your local paper each week. Don't worry if you don't understand everything to begin with; just like learning a foreign language, you'll start to pick things up before you know it. Listen to money programs on the radio, sign up to any good financial e-newsletters online and check out some of the investor magazines that come out monthly — a good one for beginners is *Money* magazine, published by ACP Magazines.

3   *Join your sisters.* Talk to any women you know to be canny investors. Even better, form a money club (which is how we got started). Just like a book club, you could arrange to meet up with friends once a month at a bar and have one member present on a finance-related topic. It's a fun way to learn, and it's amazing how motivating support from your friends can be when you're starting down the road to becoming an investor. If you really get into it, you could even start an investment group where you pool your money and buy shares together.

Investment groups on the Australian Securities Exchange website

The ASX website <www.asx.com.au> has useful information on how to start an investment group (the type where members pool money to buy shares). It also recommends various rules and regulations.

getting out of
debt and to
ground zero

There once was a girl called Joan
Who owed one hell of a loan
She scrimped and she saved
Till her debt she had paid
And boy, has her smile grown!

With so many things around to spend our money on, and with consumer marketing running amuck, it's no wonder we've become a nation of spenders, not savers. With an estimated 16 million credit cards in circulation in Australia, RBA figures show that the average credit card balance hit $3251 in December 2009 — the highest ever by Australians.

While we might not be able to convince you to curb your enthusiasm for spending money, in this chapter we'll show you how to avoid the credit trap and use your money more wisely from now on. We'll touch on how to work out what you currently own versus what you owe, and the ways in which you can get yourself out of bad debt as quickly as possible. Plus, we'll show you how to use credit to your advantage from now on — the banks might not like it, but that's just too bad! So in this chapter we'll cover:

$ where are you starting from? Working out your net worth

$ good debt versus bad debt: understanding the difference

$ getting out of bad debt: budgeting and other tricks

$ credit: making it work for you from now on.

Where are you starting from? Working out your net worth

Before you can move forward and become an investor, you should make sure you have a realistic picture of your current financial situation. To do this you'll need to work out your net worth — how much you own minus how much you owe.

• •

Try this

Calculate your net worth

Start by writing down everything you own. You should include any money you have invested in bank accounts, term deposits, superannuation, shares and property as well as any big-ticket consumer items such as a car or furniture. (Don't assume these items are worth the amount you paid for them; take a guess as to how much you'd get for them if you sold them now.)

Next, the not-so-much-fun bit: writing down everything you owe. Include any credit card debt, outstanding personal loans, your home loan, your HECS-HELP debt and any other money you owe.

Your list might look something like this:

I own: Westpac transaction account ($1500)

ING savings account ($7000)

MLC superannuation account ($32 000)

Telstra shares ($9000)

Car (resale value $8000)

Furniture (resale value $5000)

Total = $62 500

I owe: Visa card ($5000)

American Express card ($3000)

Personal loan for car ($6000)

My parents ($2000)

Total = $16 000

My net worth = $46 500 ($62 500 minus $16 000)

• •

Psst ...

Red Book

If you own a car but have no idea how much its resale value would be, check out Red Book <www.redbook.com.au> for an estimate.

If you've just realised that you have far more in the 'I owe' column than the 'I own' column and you're hyperventilating and reaching for the nearest bottle of red, relax and take a few deep breaths. There are lots of people who've been in a similar position who've worked their way out of debt into a much happier financial situation. That's the reason you're reading this book—to sort your finances out. It can be helpful to write up one of these lists every now and then (for example, every year) as it's always a good idea to keep an eye on how you're faring.

Once you have a realistic picture of where you are now, you can start planning how you're going to move forward to reach your goals. 'How am I going to do that?' you might be thinking. Simply by being smart with the money you earn. A staggering amount of the good stuff will pass through the average woman's hands over her working lifetime. In fact, a report released in 2009 by AMP and the University of Canberra estimated that a 25-year-old woman is likely to earn $1.5 million over the next 40 years (or $1.8 million if she has a bachelor degree or higher).

Being responsible with the money that comes your way over your working life will have a huge impact on your financial wellbeing. In fact, it will determine your financial future.

Good debt versus bad debt: understanding the difference

While the word 'debt' generally gets a really bad rap, there are actually two kinds of debt: good debt and bad debt — and they're very different animals.

Good debt refers to money you borrow to buy things you expect to increase in value. Taking out a mortgage to buy a property is an example of good debt.

Bad debt is any money you borrow to buy things that fall in value (things that *depreciate*). Examples include taking out a personal loan to buy a car or using your credit card to buy things such as clothes or DVDs, or to pay for holidays or evenings out.

Many of the things people purchase using credit cards and personal loans fall under the category of bad debt. Buying them might give you immediate pleasure, but they'll be worth very little (if anything) in the future. It's kind of like eating too much chocolate cake — delicious at the time, but you'll pay for it later! Not only that, if you don't pay your credit cards and personal loans off quickly, you'll find that whatever you purchased ends up costing you more than you originally paid for it due to the interest you'll have paid to the credit card or personal loan provider. Items purchased in this way fall under the category of bad debt. *Very* bad debt.

Example: Make-Believe Mary

Let's take a look at the example of Make-Believe Mary, who's taken out an $8000 personal loan to purchase a car. If it takes five years to pay the loan back at an annual interest rate of 13.99 per cent the total cost of the loan could end up being approximately $11 166, including around $3166 in interest.

Not only has Mary purchased something that after five years is worth less than she originally paid for it — but when the total interest paid is taken into account, Mary has paid far more for the car than it was worth when she originally bought it! Figures 2.1 and 2.2 (overleaf) demonstrate the difference in the overall amount of money Mary would spend if she were to pay off her loan over two years rather than five.

Huh?

Simple interest versus compound interest

The term simple interest refers to the interest that's paid on the original amount borrowed (often called the 'principal' amount). Compound interest refers to the interest paid on both the principal and any additional interest you might accrue—you'll read more about compound interest later.

Figure 2.1: paying off an $8000 personal loan over five years

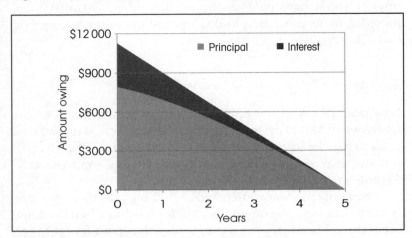

Monthly repayments: $186.10
Total amount paid: $11166 (includes $3166 in interest)

Figure 2.2: paying off an $8000 personal loan over two years

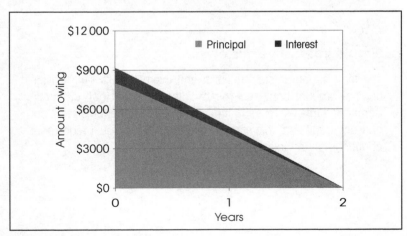

Monthly repayments: $384.07
Total amount paid: $9218 (includes $1218 in interest)

As you can see, if Make-Believe Mary could afford to increase her monthly repayments and pay off her loan in two years rather than five, she could save as much as $1900 in interest repayments.

Check out the loan repayments calculator at <www.rate detective.com.au> if you'd like to make your own calculations on personal loan interest. You'll be able to see the effect of paying them off slowly or how much you'll save in interest if you accelerate your payments and pay them more quickly.

While bad debt should be avoided whenever possible, there are ways to manage it. We'll talk about that later in the chapter.

HECS-HELP: to pay or not to pay?

HECS (the federal government's Higher Education Contribution Scheme) is now called HECS-HELP (HELP stands for Higher Education Loan Program) and it's a kind of debt that uni grad-uates over the past couple of decades will be all too familiar with. It falls under the category of good debt as it's an investment in your future and will increase your earning potential.

The question is, if you have the money, should you pay it off early or not? If you have lots of cash sitting around then it's definitely not a bad idea as the government will give you a discount for doing so — currently 10 per cent. However if you don't pay off your HECS-HELP early, it's certainly not a disaster. HECS-HELP debt does *not* attract interest and is only indexed for inflation (that is, it goes up a small percentage each year in line with the rising cost of living). Once you're working you'll only be required to start paying it back when your income surpasses the minimum threshold for compulsory repayment, and even then you won't have to come up with the money all at once — you'll simply be charged a bit extra in tax every year until you pay it off. So you should feel quite comfortable deciding to leave your HECS-HELP debt chugging along, getting rid of it slowly over the years while investing your savings elsewhere. Check out <www.goingtouni.gov.au> for full details.

Getting out of bad debt: budgeting and other tricks

If you're the proud owner of a good debt (such as a home loan) it should always be your aim to pay it all off, even if it might take you many years. However, if you have bad debt and owe money on credit cards or personal loans, your number one priority from this moment on should be to get rid of it as quickly as you possibly can. Keep your good debt humming along (if you have it) but pull out all the stops to get rid of your bad debt — pronto.

Betty's story (age 36)

My spending got out of control when I started seeing a guy a few years ago. I paid for just about everything (dinners out, concerts and movies — everything!) because he was saving for a deposit for a house for us to live in. But then we broke up. And my ex had a nice house deposit, while I had a $25 000 credit card debt. To make myself feel better about the breakup and the debt, I'd buy another pair of shoes or another dress and everything just kept getting worse.

I got into the habit of paying one credit card and then withdrawing cash from another to survive the fortnight, which only made things worse because cash withdrawals attract a higher interest rate and are the last things paid off the card. Since then, I've been making a real effort to get the debt down and it's now at $35 000 — although I've been having real problems in the last year because my payments are only making a dent in the interest. I've chopped up one card and paid off another card and closed it. I tried to get other cards with lower interest rates to swap over but didn't realise when one knocks you back, they all do. Every failed attempt to get credit is like a black mark on your credit history.

I've decided to go and see a financial adviser who'll be able to help me to work out a plan to get rid of my credit card debt once and for all — I'm really looking forward to being debt-free once again! My advice to other women? Stop buying things you really don't need. And let your boyfriend pay for his own movie tickets!

Where do you start?

So how should you go about getting out of debt? Firstly, go back and look at any debt you wrote down (the 'I owe' list) when you were reading the first part of this chapter. How many credit cards or personal loans do you owe money on? Write down the interest rate you're currently paying for each one.

You should start by paying off the credit card or personal loan on which you're paying the highest rate of interest. Obviously, you'll have to continue to make minimum payments on all of your credit cards every month, but any extra money you've saved towards clearing your debts should be put towards paying off the balance of the card or loan on which you're paying the highest interest rate. Once you've paid that off, start on the card or loan with the next highest interest rate and so on until you've finished paying them all off. If you have a number of credit cards, it's a good idea to cut them up immediately so that you stop using them. The moment you've paid each credit card off, cancel your account immediately until you have only one left. More about which credit card to keep in a minute.

Consolidating credit card debt

You could consider consolidating your credit card debt by transferring the balance of all of your cards to one card with a low rate of interest. Some cards are even interest-free to new customers for the first six months or more which, if you qualify for one, would provide you with a great opportunity to reduce your debt more quickly. It could also make your life a little simpler as you won't be juggling different cards and statements.

A word of warning: be *very* careful to read all of the fine print before you sign anything. Rarely are things free, and you might find you have to pay a fee to transfer your old cards over to a new one. Also, be careful that the interest rate on the new card won't skyrocket once the interest-free (or low-interest) period has passed. Have a look at RateCity <www.ratecity.com.au> or MoneyManager <www.moneymanager.com.au> if you're interested in finding a credit card with a low rate of interest, or if you just want to compare credit card or personal loan rates and features in general.

How are you going to pay off your debt?

Once you've worked out which credit card or loan you should be paying off first, or you've consolidated your debt, it's time to get started on the road to becoming debt free.

Using your savings to pay off debt

If you have any savings at all, you should seriously consider using this money towards clearing your bad debt. It just doesn't make sense to have $10 000 sitting in a savings account earning 5 per cent interest when you've got $8000 in credit card debt on which you're paying 18 per cent interest. You'd be far better off biting the bullet and getting rid of your debt in one fell swoop, even if you don't enjoy the prospect of seeing your savings account balance plummet. Think how good it'll feel once the slate is clear and you can start a savings plan to get yourself back on track.

If you don't have any savings or any other means of paying your bad debt in a hurry, there's only one answer: budgeting.

Budgeting to pay your way out of debt

No doubt you've turned pale at the idea, but setting yourself a budget and sticking to it doesn't condemn you to night after night of Maggi noodles for dinner — that would be a very bad idea. No, budgeting is all about being sensible with your money and making a conscious effort to spend money on what you need, rather than on everything you want — whether you're in debt or not. It's a very smart idea for everyone, and one of the key ways in which you'll build wealth.

● ●

Try this

Write down everything you spend over one month

It's important to work out how much you currently spend every month. Keep your notebook with you (or use the notes function on your mobile phone) and for one month write down everything you spend, from the little items such as a coffee or two a day, to your monthly rent or mortgage payment—and no cheating! It'll only work if you write down absolutely everything. While it might be a tedious process to go through, we urge you to do it as it's the only way you'll learn exactly where your money goes every month. And while the results might be a bit shocking, it's better you find out now that you're spending $200 per month buying your work lunches so you can do something about it. Only once you know where your money's going will you be able to work out what expenses you can cut out.

● ●

Take a look at figure 2.3 to see how small, everyday expenses can add up to a lot of money over time.

Figure 2.3: money spent on everyday expenses in one year

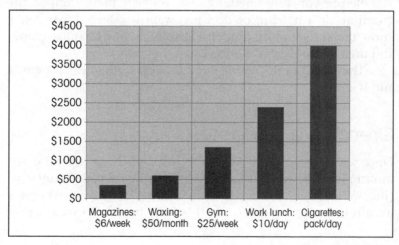

Sneaky savings

There are tons of ways in which you can save money every day. You could consider some of the following tricks to minimise your spending:

⟋   Take advantage of the specials at the supermarket every week.

⟋   Walk or ride your bike to work.

⟋   Embrace the beautician within and attempt some of your own waxing or hair dying.

⟋   Consider ditching your gym membership and taking up jogging instead.

⟋   Take your lunches to work more often.

⟋   Make sure you're on the best phone and internet plan.

⟋   Minimise your utilities bills by reducing your water and power usage whenever possible (good for the environment, too!).

There are lots of websites with savings and budgeting tips — try <www.savingsguide.com.au> for starters.

Before you buy anything, ask yourself the all-important question: do I need it, or do I just want it? Deep down you'll know the answer every time. It's absolutely fine to splurge now and then — just don't do it too often.

The moral of the story? Pay attention to the little expenses and it'll make a huge difference in the long run.

Creating a budget

Once you've got a good idea as to how much you spend every month, it's time to set up a budget. By entering your 'money in' (income) and an estimate of your 'money out' (expenses) over a month into a spreadsheet, you'll quickly be able to see roughly how much you'll be able to save every month and how much you could aim to save over a year (just multiply your monthly savings by 12). Don't forget, you're likely to spend more in some months than others (for example, when big bills such as car registration fall due). So make a note of these as obviously they'll affect how much you're able to save over the whole year.

> **Budgeting spreadsheets**
>
> There are a lot of great budgeting spreadsheets online that you can download for free. The Australian Securities and Investments Commission's consumer website, FIDO, has a very thorough budgeting spreadsheet you can fill out: <www.fido.gov.au>. Or if you've got an iPhone there are budgeting apps you can download and fill out while you're on the run—this makes it really easy to keep track of what you're spending and how you're tracking against budget.

The more you earn, the more you're likely to spend

It's a well-known phenomenon that accountants see in action all too often: people have a tendency to spend whatever they earn. So a person earning $120 000 per annum is just as likely to be living from pay cheque to pay cheque as a person who earns a more modest $45 000 per annum. Why? Because people who earn higher incomes are likely to 'reward' themselves with a more expensive lifestyle (prettier houses, fancier cars and more lavish holidays). In other words, their expenses have risen in direct proportion to their income. The trick to avoid falling into this trap is to resist upping your spending whenever you receive a pay rise and to save as much of the extra money as you can instead.

Seeking professional help to get out of debt

If you're not sleeping at night because you're struggling with debt, or if you just feel that you'd like someone to help you to set up a plan, it's time to seek the help of a professional.

A number of community organisations around Australia offer free financial counselling. Have a look at the Australian government website for Commonwealth Financial Counselling <www.fahcsia.gov.au> or try Centrelink's Financial Information Service (FIS) <www.centrelink.gov.au>. They are both free education and information services available to everyone in the community. Be aware that financial counsellors and FIS Officers are not financial advisers, and will therefore not be able to give advice or prepare a financial plan for you. They will, however, show you how to make informed decisions and help you to take control of your finances.

Alternatively, you could seek help from a licensed financial adviser — we show you where you can find one in the 'Help when you need it' section at the back of the book.

Credit: making it work for you from now on

Credit can be an extremely convenient way of managing your day-to-day expenses, as long as you use it wisely. How? By following a few simple rules. We're now going to look at the difference between credit cards and personal loans and give you some tips on using each.

Credit cards don't always have to be the work of the devil. In fact, as long as you practise self-control and don't go crazy buying things you don't need, they can be a very convenient way of using the bank's money — in some cases, completely for free. We'll show you how to make credit work for you in a minute.

Personal loans are never a good idea, and you should avoid these if at all possible. From the moment you take out the loan until you pay if off in full, you'll be paying interest — it's unavoidable — and over time this will really add up, effectively making the item you purchased cost far more than it was worth.

If there's something you want to buy (such as a car) you should always aim to save up for it first rather than taking out a personal loan. Use your self-discipline — take the bus, if necessary! If you really have no choice but to take out a personal loan, shop around. Look for the lowest rate possible, and always make sure you read the fine print and understand the terms and conditions of the loan. Ask the lender if you're not sure. Then, once you've taken out a personal loan, *get rid of it as quickly as possible.*

We've come up with eight rules to follow if you want to stop being a slave to your credit card and use it to your advantage instead:

1   *Pay your credit card balance in full every month.* If you're paying interest on your credit card purchases you're not using your card smartly. By paying off the balance in full every month you won't pay interest at all. The only fees you should be paying are the card's annual fee (if it has one) and the rewards program fee (if it's linked to the Qantas Frequent Flyer program, for example). If you choose a basic credit card that has no annual fee and isn't linked to a reward program it will be completely free to use (as long as you avoid paying interest).

2   *Never take out cash advances on your credit card.* You might be surprised to find out that if you do this, you'll often be charged a fee (based on the amount you withdraw) *plus* you'll usually start paying interest on everything that's currently waiting to be paid on your credit card from that moment on, until the balance of your card is paid off in full. Avoid this at all costs.

3   *Restrict yourself to one credit card.* There should be no reason for you to own more than one credit card, even if credit card providers do send you oh-so-enticing offers in the mail. Ignore them.

4   *Choose a credit card with a low (or no) annual fee.* Some credit cards are annual-fee-free — at least for the first six months or year. On the other hand some cards charge high annual fees, especially if they're linked with a rewards program, where you'll usually pay an extra fee for membership. If you feel you're getting your money's worth from belonging to a rewards program (perhaps you fly regularly and use your points towards free flights) then go for it. But do your sums first: it may well be that you'd never spend enough on your card to redeem anything of value and warrant paying the extra annual fee.

5   *Choose a credit card with a low interest rate.* Ideally, you'll never be paying interest again. However accidents do happen and it's only for this reason we're suggesting your credit card of choice has a low interest rate.

6   *Keep your credit limit low.* Do not be tempted to raise your credit limit, even if your lender sends you a friendly letter with an attractive-sounding offer. There are only a few instances when you should think about raising your credit limit — for example, if you're going on an overseas holiday and it'll be the easiest way of paying for things in foreign countries (rather than worrying about travellers cheques and the like). If you know you're going to be spending a lot on your card over a particular period, just make sure you'll have the funds available in your everyday transaction account to pay the balance come statement time.

7   *Check your credit card statement as soon as it arrives in the mail (or in your inbox).* If you have the stomach for it, you should write down (or enter into your mobile phone's notes tool) everything you spend on your credit card as you go, making sure you keep your receipts. Then when your statement comes in at the end of the month you should check it against your list of expenses — if there are any discrepancies, contact your card provider. Also check your statement to make sure everything is in order and you haven't been charged any incorrect interest or fees.

8   *Can't be trusted with a credit card? Get a debit card instead.* If you don't think you've got what it takes to resist spending up big on your card, think about taking out a debit card instead. You use it just like a credit card, but the money will be coming out of your everyday transaction account. This way, you won't be able to spend more than you actually have. Of course, you'll still need to keep an eye on how much you're spending.

Psst ...

Pay your credit card balance automatically

Lenders often don't openly advertise that paying off your balance in full every month is an option, and your statements will only refer to the minimum payment required every month (probably because they're making money out of you when you pay interest!). Just tell your card provider that this is what you want to do and organise for the full balance to be automatically debited from your everyday transaction account every month.

Check your credit rating

Everyone who's had some kind of credit over the past seven years will have a credit file that contains information about you and your credit history (for example, if you've ever defaulted on a loan). Credit reference agencies check out and record the credit history of potential borrowers. They then make this information available to their customers such as banks (who use information about your credit history when weighing up whether or not to offer you a loan) and utilities companies (before they set up an account for you). Obviously, you should aim to keep your credit rating as sparklingly clean as possible. You can do this by making sure that your bills are always paid in full and on time. If you'd like to check your credit rating you can do so for free at Checkmyfile <www.checkmyfile.com.au>—just click on the option for a credit report from Dun & Bradstreet, an international credit reference agency.

chapter 3

moving forward— saving is a girl's best friend

There once was a girl called Kay
Who saved part of every pay
It grew bigger and bigger
Till she gasped at the figure
And now she'll do fine come what may.

Learning how and where to save your money is important when you're getting yourself on track financially, regardless of the size of your pay cheque. While earning a lot of money could certainly make it easier to reach your goals, it doesn't necessarily follow that bringing home the big bucks will make you wealthy. Lots of people earning mega salaries live from pay cheque to pay cheque; it's just cleverly disguised behind a façade of beautiful clothes and European cars. On the other hand, many people on average salaries are often quite well off—it's just not as obvious.

The average Australian woman is in dire straits when it comes to saving. The *Women and Money Confidence Report*, commissioned and released by the ANZ bank in January 2010, showed that not only do 58 per cent of Australian women have less than $5000 in savings, but 56 per cent of women do not save money on a regular basis and one in five spend all their monthly pay cheque or regularly dip into their savings to cover living expenses.

If it sounds like this report has your name on it, don't despair. Once you've cleared your credit card debt and paid off any personal loans you might have, there are some nifty techniques you can use to get yourself on a pain-free road to saving. When you get into the habit, you'll gain momentum and find that watching the balance of your savings accounts heading north can actually give you quite a thrill — and after that, it all gets much easier. In this chapter we'll cover:

$ compound interest and paying yourself first

$ transaction accounts, savings accounts and term deposits

$ the three steps to savings glory.

Meet your new best friends: compound interest and paying yourself first

Compound interest and paying yourself first are two concepts that have been known to induce light-bulb moments in first-time investors. You wouldn't believe how simple they are, yet what a profound effect they can have on the way you think about saving and on the way in which you invest.

The concept of compound interest will make you realise that, over time, just about anything in finance land is possible; that investing isn't solely for the rich; and that you too can make your fortune.

The technique of paying yourself first will make saving and investing virtually pain free. It's a smart, low-maintenance way of building up your savings, and it's a particularly good method to use if you're the kind of person who regularly forgets to put money aside for savings and spends everything she earns instead.

So, what exactly are these concepts about?

Compound interest

Compound interest is a beautiful thing. Reputedly called 'the eighth wonder of the world' by Albert Einstein, it is simply the accumulation of interest earned on interest. In other words, compound interest occurs when you invest an amount of money and receive interest on it, then reinvest (so, roll over) your original sum of money *as well as* the interest you've earned. And so on.

For example, let's say you invest $1000 in a savings account for one year earning 5 per cent interest annually. At the end of the year, you'll have a total balance of $1050 ($1000 principal plus $50 interest). If you reinvest the total of $1050 for another year, again earning 5 per cent interest, at the end of the second year you'll have a total balance of $1102.50 ($1050 principal plus $52.50 interest). And so on.

It's the snowball effect at work, with your money (the snowball) slowly getting bigger and bigger over time as your principal and interest keep on accumulating (or in the case of the snowball, as it rolls down the hill collecting more and more snow)! This is the power of compound interest. It's quite jaw dropping how your savings will grow over time—take a look at figure 3.1 if you need convincing.

Huh?

Principal

The term 'principal' simply refers to the original amount of money (in this case, your savings) on which interest or earnings are calculated and paid by your financial institution.

The effect of compound interest

Let's say you invest $10 000, and leave it be for 40 years, earning 5 per cent interest compounding annually. How much do you think you'll have in 40 years' time? Let's have a look at figure 3.1.

Figure 3.1: effect of compound interest

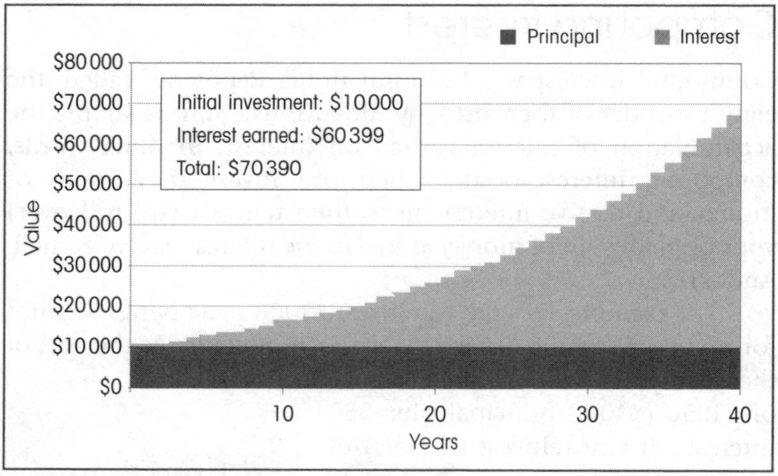

Reproduced with permission from ASIC <www.fido.asic.gov.au>.

Note: this graph assumes all interest is reinvested and doesn't take into account tax, inflation or fees.

Even though you've only invested $10 000 *and haven't added a cent more*, you would end up with more than $70 000 because of the way the interest compounds over time. Impressive, huh?

Get ready to be inspired

The effects of compound interest and time on an investment can be dramatic. Consider the following example.

Jessie and Sally are twin sisters aged 21. They have each received $5000 as a gift from their grandmother, to do with as they wish.

Jessie is very well organised, and at the age of 21 invests her $5000. She then adds $1000 every year after that until she turns 30, investing a total of $14 000 of her own money. Content with her savings effort, she adds nothing more for the next 35 years.

Sally does nothing with her inheritance until the age of 30 when she invests her $5000. Wanting to catch up to her sister, she diligently puts away $1000 for the next 35 years, contributing a total of $40 000 of her own money.

Neither Jessie nor Sally touch their interest and leave it in the bank so that compound interest can work its magic. By the age of 65, who do you think has the most savings? Check out figure 3.2 and you might be quite surprised.

Figure 3.2: Jessie and Sally's savings at 65

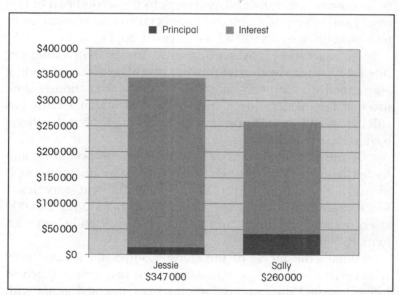

Note: this graph assumes all interest is reinvested and doesn't take into account tax, inflation or fees.

At the age of 65, you can see the different outcome for the two sisters.

Jessie:

> *Invested:* $14 000
> (Initial investment: $5000 + $9000 in contributions)
>
> *Interest earned:* $323 183
>
> *Total:* $347 183

Sally:

> *Invested:* $40 000
> (Initial investment: $5000 + $35 000 in contributions)
>
> *Interest earned:* $220 028
>
> *Total:* $260 028

Note that Sally and Jessie's investments have each earned 8 per cent growth per annum (we'll explain more about the different types of investments and their likely returns in the second part of this book) and to keep it simple, we haven't taken into account tax or fees. Nevertheless, it's still a bit of a jaw-dropper.

As you can see, by starting early and by reinvesting her interest every year, Jessie has taken full advantage of compounding and ended up with way more than Sally — even though she's invested less of her money in total. By starting later, Sally has still benefited from the power of compounding — but the effects have not been as dramatic.

If the girls hadn't taken advantage of compounding and hadn't reinvested *any* of their yearly interest at all (spending it instead), it would have been a completely different story: Jessie would have ended up at the age of 65 with only the $14 000 she'd originally invested, and Sally would have ended up with her $40 000.

What's the moral of the story? Compound interest only works when any income you earn on an investment (such as interest earned on a savings account) is reinvested along with your initial investment. This is vitally important — it might be tempting to spend your investment earnings, but you should resist this at all costs. Think about it: it's money you're currently doing without, so you shouldn't need it. Leave your investment alone and let compounding work its magic.

Lastly, the fact that you might not earn a lot of money and only be able to invest small amounts doesn't matter at all. The important thing is that you start investing as early as possible to take advantage of compounding over time. The key things to remember about compound interest are:

ſ Always reinvest any income you earn on your investment.

ſ The sooner you start investing, the less you'll need to put away.

Psst ...

Compound interest calculators

Most financial websites offer online savings calculators. These can be great for looking at the difference time, interest rates and regular contributions can have on your savings. The Australian Securities and Investments Commission (ASIC) has a particularly good one, which can be viewed at <www.fido.gov.au>.

Paying yourself first

Paying yourself first is a virtually pain-free way to build your savings over time by electing to save a specific amount of money as soon as you get paid—before you do anything else with it (and before you're tempted to spend it!).

How exactly does it work? Simply by setting up a direct debit system where a nominated amount of money is automatically transferred from your everyday transaction account to a specific savings account on a regular basis—ideally, after every pay. For example, if you're bringing home a pay cheque of $1500 a fortnight, you might set up an automatic direct debit that moves $200 into your savings account the day after your pay cheque hits your everyday transaction account. If you do this, you'll save around $5200 a year (plus any interest earned on that money).

Setting up an automatic savings system like this means you won't have to remember to move money from account to account, so it's an effort-free way of saving. And by regularly saving small amounts of money, you're unlikely to miss it. Therein lies the beauty of paying yourself first.

How much should you save? We'll talk about that later in the chapter, but the idea is that you decide on a percentage of your income (or perhaps a set regular amount to reach a specific savings goal). Remember what we've already said about compound interest: it works even with small deposits of money. Just make sure you start saving as early as possible, make regular payments and reinvest any investment earnings. By harnessing the power of compounding *and* by paying yourself first, you'll be on your way in no time. The key things to remember about paying yourself first are:

ʂ   Set up regular automatic payments to be transferred to your savings account the day after every pay day.

ʂ   Keep it going *and don't touch the money* — you're likely not to even miss it.

Transaction accounts, savings accounts and term deposits

Now that we've covered the concepts of compound interest and paying yourself first, it's time to put them into action and start saving. Before we explain exactly how to implement a savings plan, we're going to cover the difference between the various types of accounts offered by banks and building societies.

Transaction accounts are the everyday banking accounts that most people have their wage paid into. They're very convenient for managing your day-to-day finances — for example, when you need to get cash out of an ATM or pay a bill online. The downside is that they pay no, or very low, interest.

Psst ...

Avoid ATM fees

Automated teller machines are those magic holes in the wall that produce cash at the touch of a button. When you're withdrawing money, always use your own bank's ATMs. That way you shouldn't be charged a withdrawal fee (unless you go over the number of 'free' withdrawals your bank lets you make every month—keep an eye on this). If you use another bank's ATM you'll usually be slugged with a $2 fee, regardless of how much you withdraw, so avoid this whenever you can. It might not seem like much, but if you pay it regularly it'll add up over time. Wouldn't you rather use that money for something else?

Savings accounts pay higher interest rates than transaction accounts while still enabling you to access your money quickly if you need to. There can be some restrictions on the use of savings accounts (for example, you might be limited as to how many free withdrawals you can make per month) but the higher interest rate you're making on your money should more than compensate for this. In any case, once you get started you should be making deposits into your savings account—not making withdrawals!

Term deposits are similar to savings accounts, but you usually have to invest a minimum amount of money (for example, $5000 or $10 000) for which you'll generally receive a higher rate of interest. There's a catch though: you can't touch your money for a set period of time, most often anywhere from one month to five years. You usually get a higher interest rate if you're prepared to lock your money away for longer periods of time. If you find that you need to get your hands on your money before your time is up, you can generally break your term deposit—but you'll be penalised by the lender by not being paid as much interest.

Online savings accounts

Why are online savings accounts so good? Because they offer very competitive interest rates, don't usually charge any fees even if you have more than one account (so you can set up separate accounts for different savings goals) and you can organise to have money automatically transferred regularly from your everyday transaction account into your online savings account — an easy way of building up your savings. You'll also have online access so can track your savings. Bankwest, ING DIRECT and St. George Bank are some of the bigger institutions that provide online savings accounts. There are also a couple of good comparison websites you should check out when deciding which online savings account is best for you: <www.ratecity.com.au> and <www.money-au.com.au>.

Step one to savings glory: save for emergencies

The first thing you should do is to save for emergencies. This money will cover you for any unexpected events — for example, if you were to lose your job but wanted to take your time finding a new job, you wouldn't have the added pressure of worrying about money.

You should aim to save three to six months of your usual monthly expenses for emergencies (*not* your usual monthly income). Revisit the budget you wrote out while you were reading chapter 2, when you worked out how much you *spend* each month and aim to save three to six times this amount — preferably six times. It might sound like a lot, but it's very important and will be worth it — we promise.

Where should you invest your emergency savings?

In the good old days, grandma might have kept her savings under the mattress. The modern woman, however, should keep her emergency savings in a savings account or term deposit. *Do not* keep it in your everyday transaction account where it'll be indistinguishable from your spending money (for rent and bills), where you might be tempted to spend it and where you won't earn any interest on your money. Instead, choose a savings account or a term deposit with a high rate of interest. An online savings account is a great place for your emergency savings—you're usually allowed to choose a name for your accounts, so call it your 'emergency fund' (or something similar). Then leave it alone.

Step two: start saving towards your long-term and super-long-term goals

Once you've set up your emergency fund and you've reached your target (with three to six months worth of your typical expenses saved) your next step should be to start saving to fund your long-term and super-long-term goals.

You might be wondering why we'd recommend you start saving for your long-term goals before your short-term goals. By their very definition, long-term and super-long-term goals are those you'll be working towards over a long period of time—anywhere from five years to a decade, or even decades. By saving small amounts of money while you're young you won't have to save as much later due to the power of compound interest. The key is to start early: invest regularly over many years and increase your contributions in line with any pay rises you receive. The more quickly you start, the better off you'll be in the end.

What should you do first? Have a look at the long-term and super-long-term goals you wrote down while you were reading chapter 1. Perhaps you dream of owning a beautiful house someday, or a bed and breakfast. Or maybe you fancy sailing around the world on your own yacht. Whatever your goals might be, now's the time to start planning, saving and investing to reach them.

Now, the million-dollar-question: how much should you aim to save every month?

How much you save and invest for the long-term is up to you, but 10 per cent of your pre-tax pay is our suggestion. If you already have financial commitments (such as a mortgage) a smaller percentage might be more realistic. Just remember that the aim of the game is to keep on saving over many years.

Psst ...

Save 10 per cent of every pay

If you save 10 per cent of every pay (before tax), and you do so over your entire working life, you'll be setting yourself up for a very rosy financial future (and an impressive bank balance).

Where should you invest your long-term and super-long-term savings?

There are many options when it comes to investing your long-term and super-long-term savings, including the big guns, shares and property. Investing in superannuation is a particularly good idea for your super-long-term savings — we'll discuss this, as well as shares and property, in part II of the book. However, if you're young and new to investing, a great option is to open a managed fund, which can give you exposure to a range of investments including shares, property and cash.

There are a number of benefits to investing in managed funds. They're a low-maintenance type of investment where your money is managed by professionals, so they're perfect if you're time poor and want a hassle-free investment. Many funds give you the option of making regular deposits by signing up to a direct debit program where a set amount of money is deducted from your everyday transaction account every month and paid directly into your fund, which makes it easy for you to pay yourself first. Investing regularly over time and reinvesting any income that the fund generates also means you'll be taking full advantage of the power of compound interest. Exactly how do you go about investing in managed funds? We'll talk you through that in chapter 6.

You might be thinking, 'What about opening up another savings account or term deposit for my long-term savings?' While savings accounts and term deposits are a great idea for your emergency savings (that is, money you might need to get your hands on in a hurry) they aren't a good idea for your long-term savings. Why not? Because savings accounts and term deposits are cash-based investments that, over the long term, generate lower returns than other types of investment such as shares or property. Cash also loses its value over time due to the effects of inflation, making it a bad idea for long-term investments. Don't panic if this is all starting to sound a bit complicated—it will all be explained in the next chapter.

The important thing to remember when saving towards your long-term goals is that whatever type of investment you choose, you have to make regular contributions—even if they're small. The longer you keep the contributions up, the better.

Elisa's story (age 39)

I've always been told I'm a good saver. I got my first part-time job at a hairdressing salon just after I turned 15 where I was paid only $4 an hour! But for a 15 year old, that was pretty good. Living at home, everything I needed was bought for me and there wasn't really much that I wanted—so most of my weekly earnings went into my savings account. Whenever my balance reached $3000, I'd take the money out and put it into a six-month term deposit for a higher rate of interest.

Elisa's story (cont'd)

Early on, seeing friends not being able to go places or buy things because they had no money made me realise that it wasn't what I wanted for myself. Saving my money and seeing my savings grow gave me a feeling of independence that made it easy for me to stay motivated and keep saving.

When I look back I'm proud of the things I've done and experienced, and most of them have been because I've been able to save money. For example, I took a year off study between high school and university and worked in a bookstore—I saved most of that money. When I was 19, I travelled to the US for three months and spent around $10 000 of my savings on that trip. When I was 21 I bought my own car (paid for in full). When I was 27 I spent four months travelling in Europe (again, completely self-funded) and by the time I was 30 I still had around $60 000 in savings that I put towards buying a house with my husband.

My advice as a saver? Aim to save 20 to 30 per cent of your earnings and think about opening up a separate bank account to be used for saving only. Always pay your credit card balance in full every month and keep receipts to reconcile your statements. Take advantage of specials and buy things in bulk (such as movie tickets) to save a little more. Most importantly, think for yourself and buy things because you need them, not because they're fashionable or because 'everyone' has them—trends aren't trends for long.

Step three: save for your short-term and medium-term goals

Once your long-term savings plan is sorted out, it's time to start the final leg of your savings journey and think about how you're going to fund your short-term and medium-term goals — those you'd like to achieve in the next five years.

Go back to the notes you wrote while you were reading chapter 1 and remind yourself of your short-term and medium-term goals. Perhaps you want to buy a car or take an overseas vacation. Or maybe you'd like to save up for a house deposit. Work out roughly how much each goal is going to cost and how long you think it's going to take you to save up for it. You should have a fairly good idea about how much money you're capable of saving after going through this process for your emergency fund.

A word of advice: be realistic. If you realise it's going to be impossible to save for an overseas holiday *and* a new car in three years you might have to readjust your goals—don't get rid of them altogether, but either plan to give yourself more time to save or make them slightly less ambitious (for example, think about saving for a second-hand car instead of a new car).

Introducing the rule of 72

Undoubtedly something cooked up by a mathematics nerd some-where, the rule of 72 is a nifty way of working out roughly how many years it's going to take for your savings to double in value or how much interest you'll have to make in order to double your savings in a particular time (in both cases, without adding any extra money to your initial investment). The 'rule of 72' formulas are as follows.

To work out roughly how many years it's going to take for your investment to double in value:

First, you'll need to take a rough guess as to how much interest you're going to earn every year. Then, divide 72 by that number and *voila!* That's how many years it's going to take for your investment to double in value. If, for example, you think you'll earn 6 per cent interest each year, the equation would look like this:

72 ÷ 6 (your estimate of the annual interest you will earn) = 12 (years).

Introducing the rule of 72 *(cont'd)*

So if you have $1000 saved and it's earning you an average of 6 per cent interest per year it'll take 12 years before your $1000 becomes $2000.

To work out how much interest you'll have to make in order to double your money in a set period of time:

First, you'll need to work out in how many years from now you'll need your money to have doubled. Then, divide 72 by that number and Bob's your uncle — you'll have the figure for the interest rate you'll need to earn in order to make your money double in the desired amount of time. So, assuming you set a goal to double your money in 10 years, the equation would be:

72 ÷ 10 (years) = 7.2 (the average annual interest you'll have to earn to double your money).

So if in 10 years you're planning on buying a yacht to sail around the world and you currently have $50000 saved but need $100000, you must find an investment that's going to earn you an average of 7.2 per cent interest per year over the next 10 years.

Where should you invest your short-term and medium-term savings?

Savings accounts and term deposits are the go here. One of the best things you could do would be to open another online savings account (separate from your 'Emergency Fund') and set up another direct debit to transfer money into this account after every pay. You won't usually be charged a fee for having more than one account. Give it an appropriate name such as 'overseas holiday fund' or 'home deposit fund' (or both, if you've got two short-term goals and savings accounts to match) and that'll make it easy to see at a glance how your savings are faring. How much you save is up to you, but obviously you'll reach your savings goals more quickly if you cut out unnecessary expenses and save the money instead. Once you get started, momentum will kick in and it'll become easier and easier.

A final word: make sure you organise yourself. Regularly check all of your statements and file them safely away, whether or not they're on paper or electronic. It can be a real thrill when you see your savings account balances growing, and this will help to keep you motivated. You'll also need your statements come tax time— they'll show you how much money your investments have made over the last financial year and how much income you'll have to declare on your tax return.

> ### *Living Thin* by Antonia Magee
>
> *Living Thin*'s main protagonist Maggie is the Bridget Jones of personal finance. Based on the true story of an Australian woman's journey out of debt and into the heady world of saving, *Living Thin* is inspiring and a fun read to boot. (Wrightbooks, 2010.)

Tax talk

You'll have to declare any interest earned throughout the financial year on your everyday transaction account (it won't be much, if anything), savings accounts and term deposits when you complete your next tax return.

Remember: always ask for help if you need it

If you feel you need help setting up a savings plan, you should seek help from a licensed financial adviser. We tell you where you can find one in the 'Help when you need it' section at the back of the book.

chapter 4

becoming
an investor

There once was a girl called Lyn
Who, by chance, bumped into the King
His Royal Highness did sneer
'What class be you, dear?'
'Shares and cash', she replied with a grin.

Once you've started to grow your savings, it's time to think about how you're going to invest your money. This is where your money makeover really starts to ramp up and, while the ideas do begin to get more technical, it's also where they get more exciting. By investing your money wisely, you can start to make your hard-earned cash really work for you.

What you choose to invest in is very much a personal decision and will depend on your time frame, how much risk you want to take and what sort of returns you're after. Before you spring into action, you'll need to have a basic knowledge of the different asset classes and of investment concepts such as managing risk and diversification. You'll also need to understand how the ever-changing economy can have an impact on any investment you might make. In this chapter we'll cover:

$ building wealth over the long term: making your money work for you

$ the big picture: understanding risk and the economy

$ types of investments: the lowdown on asset classes

$ five top tips: how to invest for success.

Building wealth over the long term: making your money work for you

In order to build wealth over the long term, you need to make your money work hard for you. By investing some of your money in assets that grow in value over long periods of time (such as property or shares) you'll give yourself the best chance of financial success.

Why can't you just leave all your money in a bank account?

While putting some of your money in a bank account for the short term is a great idea, leaving all of your savings in the bank is not a good strategy for long-term wealth creation. It might earn you some interest, but ultimately your savings will not keep pace with the rising cost of living (also known as inflation).

For example, let's say you put $10 000 in a bank account and left it there for 20 years. When you withdraw it in the future, you might be dismayed to find that even though your account balance has increased (due to the interest it's earned) the buying power of your money has been greatly reduced. This is because the cost of living has gone up more rapidly than the value of the money you have in the bank. When investing over the long term, it's very important to ensure that your money is invested in assets that will outperform inflation. Table 4.1 shows the effect of inflation on some basic household goods over the past hundred or so years.

Table 4.1: cost of goods 1901 to 2010

Items	1901	1980	2010
Loaf of bread	2.3¢	63.8¢	$3.89
2 kg of sugar	1.3¢	95.3¢	$4.36
A dozen eggs	10.6¢	$1.47	$4.50
0.5 kg of butter	12.5¢	$1.04	$3.98

Source: Australian Bureau of Statistics (1901, 1980)

Before you start to impersonate your nanna bemoaning the terrible price of things these days, keep in mind that the average weekly salary in 1901 was $4.35 a week!

The Reserve Bank of Australia generally tries to keep inflation between 2 and 3 per cent per year. If you're curious to know why keeping inflation under control is such a big deal, take poor old Zimbabwe as an example of inflation gone crazy. In 2008 it was estimated that inflation climbed to between 231 million per cent and 89.7 sextillion (yes, that's with 21 zeros after it) per cent as the government continued to print new denominations of money (including a $100 billion note) to pay off international debt. It was widely reported that many Zimbabweans needed to hold billions of dollars just to carry out simple transactions such as buying household groceries.

Huh?

Inflation

Remember way back, when you could buy a massive bag of mixed lollies from your corner store for only 20 cents? Well now you'd be forking out a disgraceful two dollars or more for the same bag! That's the impact of inflation for you. Inflation is a term used to demonstrate the overall increase in price of all goods and services over time.

Huh?

Capital growth and capital gains tax

Capital growth is just a fancy-pants name for how much profit you make on something. For example, if you buy a cheap iPod on eBay for $100 then sell it to your brother for $150, you've made a capital gain of $50 (that is, you have $50 more capital than when you began). Note that capital growth will attract capital gains tax—another name for tax you'll pay on any money your investment has made.

Investment strategies

Now that you understand why your investments need to outperform inflation, it's time to learn how you can make this happen. Here's an overview of three ways in which you can invest to make your money work for you in the longer term:

1   *Investing for capital growth.* The aim here is to invest in assets such as property and shares that increase in value over time. For example, if you buy a house for $400 000 and then sell it five years later for $500 000, your asset has grown by $100 000 — in other words, you've achieved 25 per cent capital growth. Investing for capital growth is great for younger people who have time on their side to let the asset grow without having to stress out if it goes up and down in value over the short term.

2   *Investing to create income.* Investments will often provide you with regular payments, or income. Income-yielding investments include:

  → cash (where you get income in the form of interest)

  → shares (where you can receive income in the form of dividends)

→ investment property (where you'll receive income in the form of rent).

We will talk about shares and property in more detail later on.

3 *Borrowing money to make money.* When you borrow money to invest, you're taking advantage of gearing. The most common form of gearing is to borrow money from the bank to buy a property (so to take out a mortgage), but you can borrow money to invest in shares or managed funds too. Gearing gives you the opportunity to make much more money than you could ever make on your own, but it also increases your risk of losing money. The day will come when you have to pay back the loan and, if the investment is not going as well as you'd expected, it could mean that you have to sell your investment at a loss.

Tax talk

Different investments come with different tax implications. You should make sure you fully understand how tax applies to any investment you make so you don't get any nasty shocks come tax time. Some investments offer great tax advantages, which can be super helpful when building your portfolio. We outline how tax impacts on the major forms of investment (shares, managed funds, superannuation and property) in part II of this book.

Huh?

Growth assets

Growth assets (which include some types of property and shares) are assets that increase in capital value *and* produce income. They can also have some great tax advantages.

Karina's story (age 42)

When I was in my early 20s, Mum gave my brothers and me a small sum of money each to invest when she sold the family business. That's when I got interested in shares. Mum and I started going to ASX information sessions and I found a stockbroker who kickstarted my portfolio.

Things were going well until my de facto of seven years and I split up. To my surprise, I had banks chasing me for his unpaid loans—the existence of which he'd been hiding for years. I had virtually no assets other than my share portfolio, I was facing a job redundancy and was living in expensive Sydney. This was a real turning point for me. I took a job transfer, and put all my energy into repaying the debts and saving.

A few years later I'd scraped together a deposit for a property. I started househunting every weekend for a place that was within my budget and that met my simple criteria of two bedrooms, parking, and in an area that was no more than a $20 taxi ride from where I liked to go out. I eventually found what I was looking for, and four years later I sold the property at a 40 per cent profit with no capital gains tax (as I'd been living in it myself). I could never have saved that much money in that short a space of time. I am now in the process of educating myself about investing and building a property portfolio so I'll be less reliant on monthly pay cheques from an employer. I'm also continuing to build my wealth in shares and cash savings.

What I've learnt is that it's okay to take risks, as long as you've educated yourself and you're not just gambling. It's also important to make your money work for you and not be a slave to your salary. Just saving money is a poor way of building wealth as bank deposit interest is often lower than the rising cost of living. Nothing frustrates me more than watching my female friends ignoring the most important road to freedom by not making their money work for them. My advice is to find an area of investment you can understand and dip your toe in the water. It's not as scary as you think.

The big picture: understanding risk and the economy

When deciding how to invest your money, there are two important things to consider: how long you want to invest for, and how much risk you're willing to take.

The key to making good decisions about how to invest your money is to understand how long you should aim to hold your money in each type of investment (or asset class) in order to reduce your level of risk. For example, international shares have historically generated very high returns, but they're considered a risky investment due to the short-term volatility of sharemarkets around the world. This makes international shares much more suitable as a long-term investment option than a short-term one. We'll go into detail about the level of risk each investment attracts soon.

It's also important to remember that *all* investments come with a level of risk attached. As an investor, you need to understand that risk is a fundamental part of investing, and rather than avoid it you should understand and manage it.

Australian Securities and Investments Commission (ASIC) — *Investing between the flags*

ASIC has put out a great document that's all about how to manage risk and invest safely. It's called *Investing between the flags* and you can download it from its website, <www.fido.gov.au>.

Once you've accepted that investing always involves a little bit of risk and you know that different types of investment are better suited to different time frames, think about your goals and personal circumstances in order to best pick an investment to suit you. It's no good choosing a high-return but high-risk investment if you're losing sleep at night. On the other hand, it's not smart to leave your money in a bank account for 10 years earning low interest either — due to the effects of inflation that's a high-risk move too.

Psst ...

Ignore emails from Nigerian millionaires

Be suspicious of any investments tempting you with talk of riches and guaranteed high profits (or emails asking you to help transfer millions of dollars for a 'worthy cause' in Africa, for that matter). If someone is promising you higher than average returns, be very suspicious — get-rich-quick schemes rarely work.

How the economy affects you

Being part of a global community means that everything is interlinked in weird and wonderful ways. This means your investments will be influenced by many things outside of your control, ranging from government announcements to natural disasters. For example, in the week following September 11 both the US and Australian sharemarkets plummeted. In particular, share prices for airline and insurance companies fell significantly as a result of investors predicting these industries would be hard hit and become less profitable following the attacks. While the inevitability of unpredictable events makes it impossible for even the best economists to predict what's going to happen next, there are key trends that can be helpful when trying to understand how broader economic or social trends will affect your investments.

Key indicators: things to watch out for

While you don't need an economics degree to be a great investor, it can be useful to understand some of the basic key economic indicators and how they might influence your investments. This knowledge can help you make more informed investment decisions. Four indicators to keep an ear out for are the consumer price index, interest rates, gross domestic product and the federal budget.

The Consumer Price Index

The Consumer Price Index (CPI) reflects the overall change in the average cost of consumer goods and services, and is one of the most keenly watched economic indicators. Any change in CPI is expressed as a percentage and is published by the Australian Bureau of Statistics (ABS). It's regarded by most analysts as being the key measure of inflation. An increase in CPI means that inflation is on the rise, and it will take more of your dollars to purchase the same set of basic consumer items. The Reserve Bank of Australia (RBA) keeps an eagle eye on CPI and adjusts interest rates accordingly (more about that below). One of the reasons it's important for investors to keep track of CPI is to ensure the return on their investments outperforms the inflation rate over time. For example, you don't want to hit retirement down the track, only to find that your superannuation balance hasn't kept ahead of CPI growth and you can't afford basic items (when a dozen eggs costs $20 at some point!).

Interest rates

Interest is the fee charged by a lender to someone who borrows their money. Interest rates are expressed as a percentage of the sum borrowed. On the first Tuesday of every month (except January), home owners and the media wait in eager anticipation for interest rate announcements by the Reserve Bank of Australia (RBA). The RBA is the central monetary authority for the Australian economy and it uses interest rates as a lever to control consumer spending and keep debt and inflation under control — its mission is to keep inflation between 2 and 3 per cent. For example, to slow the economy down the RBA will put interest rates up so that consumers start spending less. Interest rates affect almost everyone as they impact on repayments on mortgages, loans and credit cards. They also affect the profits of companies who have debt or investments. They can be unpredictable — it's interesting to note that while the average standard variable home loan interest rate between 2000 and

2010 was around 7.2 per cent, in the years of shoulder pads and bad perms in the '80s they got as high as 17 per cent. Interest rate movements have big implications for investors. For example, if you own property and the RBA announce a rise in interest rates, it's highly likely your bank will follow suit and you'll need to fork out more dosh on your mortgage repayment (if you have a variable interest loan) each month.

Organisations to keep an eye on

Keep an eye out for mention of the following organisations in the news, as they regularly make announcements and release interesting facts and figures that indicate how the economy is faring:

→   The Australian Bureau of Statistics
→   The Reserve Bank of Australia
→   The Federal Government
→   The US Federal Reserve
→   The US Treasury.

Gross Domestic Product

Gross Domestic Product (GDP) refers to a country's overall economic output and is considered the broadest benchmark of the health of the economy. In simple terms, the GDP is the market value of all goods and services that are produced within Australia. Australia's GDP figures are released every quarter by the ABS. Positive GDP figures mean the economy has expanded or grown, but if Australia has two quarters of negative GDP in a row it's officially considered to be in recession. By looking at the movement of GDP over a number of quarters, investors can determine whether the economy is trending upward or downward and in turn understand how their investments might be affected. For example, if you own shares in a retail company, and there is an economic downturn, you can anticipate that your shares may not fare so well if consumers rein in their spending.

The federal budget

Each year around May, financial and political nerds go nuts when the federal treasurer announces the budget. The budget is a document outlining how the government believes the economy is faring and what plans it has in place for tax, spending and other initiatives. This, like any major announcement, will have some effect on sharemarkets depending on how investors react.

Trends: it's all just a little bit of history repeating

While you can't predict exactly what's going to happen with the economy, there is evidence to suggest that everything runs in cycles. The theory of the economic clock was first published in London's *Evening Standard* in 1937, but even today it's commonly used in investment publications to try to predict the direction the economy will take. The idea is that everything happens in a particular pattern and that some assets perform better than other assets at certain times in the economic cycle. Figure 4.1 shows how economic events occur in a cyclical order.

Figure 4.1: the economic clock

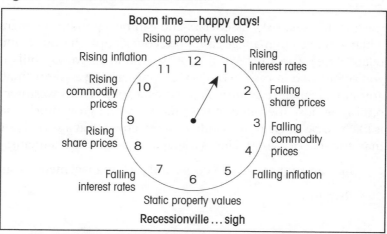

Source: Roger Kinsky, *Teach Yourself About Shares.*

It's estimated a full cycle takes between seven and nine years to complete, however there's no scientific way to measure exactly how long a full cycle takes, or how long it takes to get from one part of the cycle to the next — we might all be rich if there were! However it does demonstrate that throughout history, recessions have eventually ended — so there's no need to hit the panic button when we fall into one.

Types of investments: the lowdown on asset classes

There are a ludicrous number of ways to invest your money, but pretty much all of them fit into four broad categories known in the financial world as asset classes. Each asset class has a different level of risk and a different potential return. You'll need to familiarise yourself with the different asset classes, as you'll hear them mentioned everywhere from your superannuation statements to any financial publication you might come across. Asset classes are broadly defined as: cash, fixed interest, property and shares. Each will be discussed in detail in the following pages.

Cash

Cash is the least risky asset class and can be a good investment when you need to manage cash flow. For example, it's quick and relatively easy to move your money around or to pay bills if you've invested in cash. However, despite earning a (very) small amount of interest, cash isn't great as a long-term investment option because the value of your money won't grow much and is likely to be eaten away by inflation (by growing at a slower rate than the cost of living). Here's a snapshot of cash investments:

$ *Includes*: transaction accounts and cash management trusts

$ *Risk*: low

$ *Average return over the long term*: low (0 to 1 per cent after inflation)

$ *How you make money*: income via interest

$ *Typical investment time frame*: short term (zero to three years).

Your cash is only as secure as the organisation in which it's invested

While cash is considered the most secure type of investment you should be aware that it's only as good as the organisation you invest it in. Exhibit A: one Mr Charles Ponzi.

In the 1920s in Boston, Mr Ponzi became a millionaire by promising investors 50 per cent interest on cash investments in 45 days. Over 4000 people invested 15 million dollars in total. What they didn't know was that their returns were taken either from their own or other people's money, rather than any profit earned. When the scheme eventually came crashing down, investors only received 30 cents for every dollar they invested.

Similar operations are now commonly known as 'Ponzi schemes'. And yes, they still exist—even in Australia. If you took part in the Ponzi scheme operated by Giuseppe Mercorella in South Australia in 2007 (who was offering 36 per cent return a year) you may have been among the investors who lost a total of 79 million dollars. The moral of the story? Invest your money only in reputable institutions or businesses that you fully understand.

Fixed interest

Fixed interest is another low-risk investment category where you invest for a specific length of time, at an agreed rate of interest. It can be a good strategy for achieving your short-term goals, such as saving for a car you're aiming to buy in three years. Like cash, fixed interest is fairly secure but over the long term your money may not keep pace with inflation. Here's a snapshot of fixed interest investments:

§   *Includes*: savings accounts, term deposits and local and international government bonds.

§   *Risk:* low to medium.

§   *Average return over the long term:* low (0 to 3 per cent after inflation).

§   *How you make money*: income via interest.

§   *Typical investment time frame:* short- to medium-term (zero to five years).

Property

Property is viewed as a medium- to high-risk investment because, depending on the type of property, it can go up and down in value in the short term. However, property can give you good capital growth over longer periods of time and can generate additional income if, for example, you have a rental property. You can also invest in property on the sharemarket through a listed property trust, where you invest in a company that invests in commercial real estate. Here's a snapshot of property investments:

§   *Includes*: residential and commercial property plus listed property trusts.

§   *Risk:* medium to high.

§   *Average return over the long term*: 1 to 3 per cent for residential and 3 to 5 per cent for commercial property (after inflation).

§   *How you make money*: capital growth and possibly income (if you rent out a property).

ſ   *Typical investment time frame*: short-term (if you're buying
    to renovate and sell quickly) to long-term (if you're
    buying a family home to live in or building up a property
    portfolio).

Shares

Shares are considered high risk because they swing up and down
in value in the short term. They do, however, have the potential
to bring high returns over the long term. This category includes
both Australian and international shares, with international
shares usually considered a higher risk investment than Australian
shares. Here's a snapshot of share investments:

ſ   *Includes:* Australian and international shares.

ſ   *Risk:* high.

ſ   *Average return over the long term*: 5 to 8 per cent for
    Australian shares and 6 to 9 per cent for international
    shares (after inflation).

ſ   *How you make money*: capital growth and possibly income
    (if the shares offer dividends).

ſ   *Typical investment time frame*: long-term (over five years).

Risk versus return

As you can see, each asset class and investment type offers
different levels of risk and potential return. Generally, the higher
the return the more volatile the investment is in the short term.
However, if you take a long-term perspective, higher risk can
mean higher returns — as long as you can live with the inevitable
ups and downs in the meantime. Before investing, you need to
work out what level of risk you are comfortable with and ensure
it fits with your financial goals. Figure 4.2 (overleaf) shows the
correlation between risk and return over different asset classes.

Figure 4.2: risk versus return

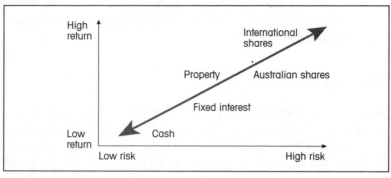

The golden rule: don't put all your eggs in one basket

One of the most important principles of investment is diversification — the 'don't put all your eggs in the one basket' technique. History shows us that different asset classes perform strongly or poorly at different times, so having your money spread across different asset classes is a great way to minimise your risk and protect your portfolio. While one asset class might be performing poorly (shares might be having a bad year, for example) another may be doing well — so your investments balance themselves out. Check out table 4.2 to see how the major asset classes have each performed every year over the past 17 years.

Table 4.2: annual asset class returns to 30 June 2009 (%)

Yearly to 30 June	Cash	Fixed interest	Australian shares	Global shares	Australian listed property	CPI
1993	5.91	13.93	9.91	32.58	17.67	2.2
1994	4.93	-1.13	18.46	0.43	7.96	2.2
1995	7.10	11.88	5.71	14.74	8.87	2.7
1996	7.75	9.45	15.83	7.15	3.55	2.8
1997	6.77	16.76	26.56	29.11	29.29	2.1

Yearly to 30 June	Cash	Fixed interest	Australian shares	Global shares	Australian listed property	CPI
1998	5.11	10.88	1.64	42.68	10.21	1.9
1999	5.04	3.28	15.34	8.54	3.11	1.6
2000	5.58	6.17	15.06	24.17	16.62	2.7
2001	6.08	7.42	9.11	-5.67	13.90	3.0
2002	4.66	6.21	-4.54	-23.21	14.85	2.8
2003	4.97	9.78	-1.61	-18.15	12.15	2.7
2004	5.30	2.33	21.73	19.90	17.24	2.5
2005	5.56	7.79	26.03	0.53	18.10	2.6
2006	5.85	3.41	24.02	20.44	18.05	2.8
2007	6.42	3.99	29.21	8.27	25.87	2.7
2008	7.34	4.42	-13.67	-20.84	-36.35	4.3
2009	5.48	10.82	-20.34	-15.66	-42.27	3.6

© Lonsec Limited. Source: Lonsec/Morningstar/Reserve Bank of Australia.

Note: highest annual returns are shaded. Cash: UBS Warburg Bank 0 + years. Fixed interest: Australia UBS Warburg Composite 0 + years. Australian shares: Australian S&P/ASX All Ordinaries Accumulation Index. Global shares: Global MSCI World Accumulation Index with Gross Div ($A). Property: Australian S&P/ASX 300 Property Trust Accumulation Index.

Allocating your assets

Once you've understood the principle of diversification, it's time to work out what proportion of your money you should place in each asset class. This is referred to as your 'asset allocation'. For example, do you put a high proportion of your available funds into shares, and a low proportion in cash, or the other way around?

You might be thinking, 'I'm just getting started — how on earth can I invest in all of the asset classes, let alone work out what percentage to put where?' Don't stress out. Of course you can't do it all straight away. It'll take time for you to understand it all then build up a portfolio. Even then the best investors tweak their portfolios over time as their investments grow and their goals change.

To start with, you really need to look back at your goals and assess your whole financial picture. Ask yourself the following questions:

$ How much cash do I have in my savings accounts?

$ What other investments do I own (including superannuation)?

$ What do I want my next investment to be?

Answering these questions will give you a starting point as to how best allocate your assets and avoid putting all your eggs in one basket. For example, if most of your money is sitting in a term deposit you could consider starting a share portfolio next or putting a portion of your cash towards a property purchase.

Part II of the book explains your investment options in depth, so you'll start to get a clearer picture about what you might like to invest in.

Remember, you're not alone

When you really get into it and your investments start to grow, you might find you need help with your asset allocation to ensure you have the right mix. Luckily there are professionals who can help. For example, you could consider seeing a licensed financial adviser for help with assessing your financial situation.

Five top tips: how to invest for success

While you can't control the economy or predict which way the markets or property prices might be heading there are some things you can do in order to make the most of your investments. Here are our top five tips on how to invest for success:

1   *Understand what you're doing.* Make sure you fully understand what you're investing in. Be suspicious of any person or company promising you the secret to fast and easy riches.

Make sure you're also aware of any fees you might be paying — they can add up over time and make a massive difference to your future returns. Fine-print reading required!

2   *Know yourself and the environment.* You need to understand how much risk you're prepared to take in order to meet your goals. Keep in mind that the amount of risk you take should be considered in light of your investment time frame. An investment that might be risky in the short term (such as shares) might be a sensible investment choice for the long term, and vice versa. By understanding how the economy works, you can look out for trends that can help inform your investment choices.

3   *Spread the love.* Diversifying your investments is one of the fundamental keys to successful investing. Different types of investments go up under certain economic conditions, while others go down. By investing across the different asset classes, no single investment should cause you too much grief.

4   *Give it time.* There's a common financial saying: 'It's time in the markets, not timing the markets that counts.' Investments run in cycles, so instead of trying to work out when to buy and sell all the time (which even the professionals find hard to do accurately), hold your growth investments over the long term. You'll minimise your risk and give yourself the best chance of financial success.

5   *Take advice.* If you don't have the time, energy or confidence to invest on your own, consider seeing a licensed financial adviser who'll help you put a plan together. Be sure to ask for one who bills by fee for service rather than being commission based so you know that any advice you receive is unbiased. We'll tell you where you can find one in the 'Help when you need it' section later in the book.

part II
choose your own adventure

So, you've paid off any outstanding debts and have hit ground zero. You've put together a budget, are merrily saving away and you're fully prepped about becoming an investor. Now it's time for the fun part of your money makeover: choosing your investment weapon of choice.

The investment weapon (or weapons) you choose will depend on a number of things, including your age, how long you want to invest for, what you want to achieve and simply what type of investment floats your boat. Some people love the idea of becoming a property mogul, while others prefer the excitement of the sharemarket. Then there are those who declare that superannuation, with its tax advantages, is one of the best investment choices of all. Remember, over time you can (and should) invest in more than one thing—diversifying is one of the fundamental keys to minimising risk and securing your future riches.

In the next four chapters you'll explore the ins and outs of investing in:

$ shares

$ managed funds

$ superannuation

$ property.

Buckle up and get ready to enter the dynamic world of investing.

chapter 5

shares

There once was a girl called Laura
Whose work life was starting to bore her
She decided to trade
Lots of money she made
Now she spends all her days in Majorca.

To an outsider, the world of the sharemarket looks fast and exciting. You've probably seen scenes of the traders on the floor of the New York Stock Exchange frantically running around, adrenaline fuelled. While in reality you probably won't find yourself yelling 'sell, sell, *sell!*' down your phone to your broker (sadly, in Australia, the trading floor is really just a giant computer), shares remain a dynamic way to invest — and they're not necessarily as risky as the press might have us believe. In fact, the Australian sharemarket has historically made excellent returns over the long term. Shares can also be a good starting point for your money makeover if you don't want the commitment (or have the money) required to invest in property.

Many women hesitate before buying shares because they don't know enough about the sharemarket, or are unsure if it's the right time to buy. Truth be told, it's less intimidating than you might think, and really comes down to one thing: research — knowing what to look for and where to find the information you need. Plus, you already have a natural advantage as a woman — studies have shown that women who invest in the sharemarket make better returns than men, and fewer mistakes — we act with less bravado and are much more likely to research and seek advice. In this chapter we'll cover:

§ shares 101: what is the sharemarket and how does it work?

§ buying and selling shares: the aim of the game

§ the big six: what to look for when investing in shares

§ checklist: getting ready to buy shares.

At a glance

Here's a snapshot of six things you might like to know about investing in shares:

→ **Who is best suited to investing in shares?** People who enjoy research and who want control over their investment.

→ **How much money do I need to start?** You can buy a parcel of shares with around $500 (but $5000 is much better!).

→ **How much money can I expect to make?** It varies and depends on the type of company you invest in, the time frame and how much risk you want to take. As an indication, the Vanguard Index Chart 2009 states that Australian shares as a whole have returned an average of 9.2 per cent per year over the past 20 years (not taking inflation into account). In other words, if you invested $10000 across the Australian sharemarket in 1989 and reinvested your dividends, by 2009 it would be worth over $58000.

→ **What kind of time frame works best for investing in shares?** A minimum of five years is recommended for long-term share investors.

→ **How much work goes into investing in shares?** For long-term investors, a large chunk of research will come upfront. After that, shares are fairly low-maintenance.

→ **Look out for:** 'tips' from Uncle Bob. He might be a whiz under the bonnet, but how much does he really know about investing?

Shares 101: what is the sharemarket and how does it work?

A basic understanding of how the sharemarket works is essential for anyone looking to become financially savvy. The share-market is fundamentally linked to how our economy works and underpins almost every investment you might make. For example, your superannuation fund will almost certainly invest some of your money in shares. This means that when the sharemarket goes up or down, your superannuation fund is likely to go up and down in value too.

What exactly is a share?

A company that wants to set up a new business or expand its existing business may be able to raise the money it needs to do this by becoming a listed company on the stock exchange and issuing shares to the general public (that is, you!). Not every company can, or wants, to become listed — indeed most aren't.

To become listed, a company needs to meet certain criteria to do with their size and profitability. For example, they need to have earned over one million dollars in pre-tax profits over the past three years and have a minimum number of shareholders (around 500 investors). Once a company has been listed on the stock exchange it must adhere to certain rules and regulations, such as informing the market if there have been any changes to the business that might affect the share price.

If you buy a share in a company, you essentially become a part owner in the business and the share you've purchased is proof of your ownership. For the record, shares can also be called stocks, securities or equities.

What is the sharemarket?

A sharemarket is the place where shares are bought and sold. Think of it as a massive-scale version of your local market filled with various stalls offering different shares to buy or sell.

In Australia, the main sharemarket is called the ASX — the Australian Securities Exchange, previously called the Australian Stock Exchange. Companies on the ASX are divided into 10 different sectors, including the financial sector (which includes companies such as the Commonwealth Bank), the telecommunications sector (which includes companies such as Telstra) and the consumer staples sector (which includes companies such as Woolworths).

It's interesting to note that Australian shares only make up 2 per cent of the global sharemarkets. You are able to invest directly in overseas companies through overseas exchanges and sharemarkets, but it's much harder to do the necessary research and properly manage the currency risk. This is why most beginner investors tend to stick to the ASX or choose to buy international shares through a managed fund (which we'll talk about in our next chapter).

Just how big is the ASX?

There are more than 2000 companies currently listed on the ASX with a combined total value of over a trillion dollars. This makes it one of the world's top 10 largest sharemarkets.

What are the All Ordinaries?

This is finance gobbledegook at its best: you'll often hear news reporters or finance experts talking about what's happening with the All Ordinaries, Dow Jones, Hang Seng and so on. These names simply represent a sample group (or index, in finance-speak) of companies in a particular country that are used to give an indication of how that particular sharemarket as a whole is performing.

For example, the All Ordinaries is one of the Australian sharemarket's best-known benchmark indexes, comprising approximately 500 of the largest companies actively traded on the ASX. If you hear on the news that the 'All Ords' are up by 20 points at the close of the day's trade, it means that, on average, those 500 Australian companies are doing slightly better than they were on the previous day.

Another well-known benchmark index in Australia is the S&P/ASX 200. S&P stands for Standard and Poor's, which is a global company that publishes financial research and analysis on shares. It's also well known for its sharemarket indices, including the S&P/ASX 200 — a group of the largest 200 companies on the Australian sharemarket. The S&P/ASX 200 index has now overtaken the All Ordinaries as the most common benchmark index for the Australian sharemarket. Overseas equivalents are the Dow Jones (US), the FTSE (pronounced 'footsie' — UK), the Hang Seng (Hong Kong) and the Nikkei (Japan).

How you make money from shares

When you buy shares in a company you're aiming for one (or both) of the following two things: growth and income. Let's have a closer look at each one.

Growth

If you invest in shares for growth, you're hoping that the share price rises over time. So you buy a share for $10, the price rises to $20 and voila — you've doubled the value of your investment. Of course it can work the other way, too, and the value of your investment will decrease if the share price goes down. Owning shares that rise in value allows you to grow your investment, like buying a good bottle of wine that gets better with age.

Remember, like any marketplace, the sharemarket operates on the principle of supply and demand. The more people who want to buy a particular share, the higher the price will go. The more people who want to sell a share, the lower it will go. A share price is determined largely by the market's perception of a company's current performance and its future potential.

As an indication, Australian shares as a whole have traditionally grown over the long-term and made excellent returns. According to the *Vanguard Index Chart 2009*, if you'd invested $10 000 in shares across the Australian sharemarket in 1970, by the end of 2009 the value of those shares would now be worth over $453 000. Got your attention now, huh? Even if we go back to day dot, the Australian sharemarket has averaged 7.5 per cent return per year *after inflation*, even taking into account market crashes.

Income

You might also invest in shares to provide a regular income from dividends. As an incentive to shareholders, some companies (but not all) choose to distribute some of their profits to shareholders in the form of dividends.

Dividend amounts, sometimes called yields, vary depending on the company and generally range somewhere between 2 and 8 per cent of the overall share price. It all depends on whether a company prefers to use its profits to grow the business, or to pay a higher dividend to its shareholders. You can take your dividends as cash or reinvest them and purchase additional shares if the company you own shares in offers a dividend reinvestment scheme.

For example, if you had shares in the National Bank of Australia in December 2009 you would have received a 73 cent dividend for each share you owned. So if you had 100 shares (valued at $27.74 each at the time) you would have received $73.

Huh?
Dividends

Happy days! A dividend is a regular payment a company takes from its profits and gives to its shareholders to reward them and attract future investors. Companies generally pay dividends every six or 12 months. The amount paid per share is decided by the company's board of directors.

Are shares risky?

Just like Britney Spears, shares often get bad press. Emotive words such as 'crash' and 'plummet' are used in relation to sharemarket movements and this makes investing in shares appear oh-so risky.

There's no doubt that investing in shares (particularly over the short term) involves risk. Prices are affected by many things outside your control — interest rates, inflation and the value of the dollar, to name a few. But despite this short-term volatility Australian shares as a whole have risen over the long term.

While it's not possible to predict the future or know exactly what's around the corner, we can look to the past to know that the Australian economy (and the sharemarket) has always recovered after a downturn, even after the Great Depression of the 1930s and two World Wars. Nobody knows when there'll be a downturn, but if history is anything to go by there'll be plenty more. However, history also shows that the odds that the sharemarket will recover are good, so your investments will more than likely recover, too, if you take care to invest wisely and minimise your risk.

Figures 5.1 and 5.2 show how Australian shares have performed historically.

Figure 5.1: Australian shares since 1900

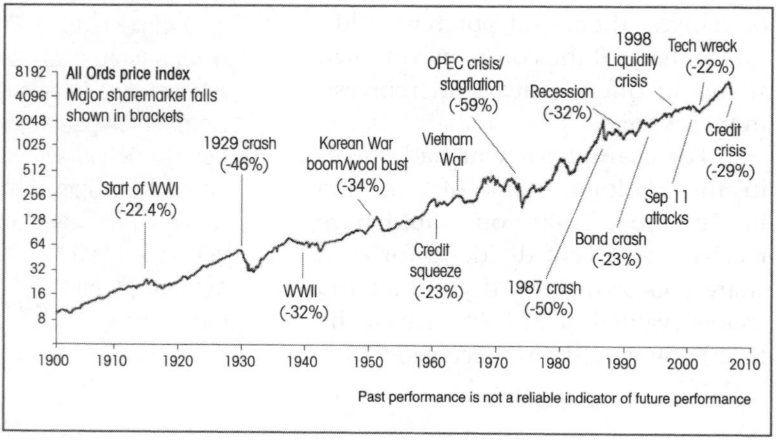

Reproduced with permission from QSuper.

$Psst$ ...

Free sharemarket chart

Go to the ASX website <www.asx.com.au> and download the *Australian share price movement chart*. The chart shows all movements of the Australian sharemarket since 1900 and lists the major historical events that drove the share price higher or lower.

Figure 5.2: Australian sharemarket returns 1950 to 2009

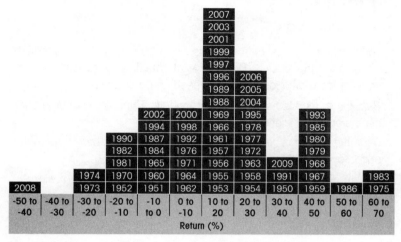

-50 to -40	-40 to -30	-30 to -20	-20 to -10	-10 to 0	0 to 10	10 to 20	20 to 30	30 to 40	40 to 50	50 to 60	60 to 70
						2007					
						2003					
						2001					
						1999					
						1997					
						1996	2006				
						1989	2005				
						1988	2004				
				2002	2000	1969	1995		1993		
				1994	1998	1966	1978		1985		
			1990	1987	1992	1961	1977		1980		
			1982	1984	1976	1957	1972		1979		
			1981	1965	1971	1956	1963	2009	1968		
		1974	1970	1960	1964	1955	1958	1991	1967		1983
2008	1973	1952	1951	1962	1953	1954	1950	1959		1986	1975

Return (%)

Source: JP Morgan, Perennial Investment Partners to 31 December 2009.

Minimising risk

Investing in shares doesn't have to mean you spend your spare time chewing your nails stressing out about losing your money. Like all investments, investing in the sharemarket does carry an element of risk — but you can minimise it by doing the following simple things.

Researching

Research potential companies thoroughly and only invest in those that have historically demonstrated strong returns with all signs pointing to a profitable future. Some indicators to consider when doing your research include whether they are a market leader (for example, they are in the top 100 companies on the ASX), if they have limited competition for their product or service, and if they have shown a consistently strong rate of return over the past five or more years.

Huh?

Bulls and bears

You'll hear the words 'bull' or 'bullish' and 'bear' or 'bearish' bandied about investing circles. Do not be alarmed! They simply refer to whether the market as a whole is heading up or down.

Bull: the market is heading up as a whole. Think: bulls charge and people enter the market for action.

Bear: the market is heading down as a whole. Think: bears hibernate and people leave the market to sleep.

Diversifying

Invest in shares across different asset classes to spread your risk around. Remember, different asset classes do better than others at different times in the economic cycle. By investing across different asset classes, you don't need to worry as much if some of your shares go down, because hopefully others will be going up at the same time. Also, if one company doesn't do so well, it won't create too many premature grey hairs.

Adopting a medium-to-long-term outlook

Investing for five or more years can help minimise the impact of short-term volatility in the sharemarket because it gives your shares time to recover from a downturn.

Huh?

Liquidity

'Liquidity' is just a fancy-pants term to describe how quickly you'll get your hands on the money from your investment if you sell it.

The good, the bad and the ugly

Here are some pluses and minuses to consider when investing in shares.

The good:

$ *Financial control.* You have the flexibility to buy or sell shares whenever you like, in whichever company you like. This means that shares have a high level of liquidity compared with an investment such as residential property, which could take you months and months to sell.

$ *Minimal fees.* Shares have comparatively low administrative fees (you can buy a parcel of shares online from as little as $15) compared with those charged by managed funds (which you'll read about in chapter 6).

$ *Tax benefits.* Shares can enjoy good tax benefits, particularly if you invest in an Australian company that offers franked dividends. Although you'll have to pay capital gains tax (that is, tax on any profit you make when you sell the shares), if you hold the shares for over 12 months you'll only have to pay tax on 50 per cent of your profit.

Huh?

Franked dividends

Dividends from some Australian companies can be franked. A franked dividend is a dividend on which the company has already paid part or all of the company tax. It can be fully franked or partially franked, but either way you'll receive a tax imputation or tax credit along with the dividend, which means you pay less when the tax man comes calling. In other words, franked dividend = less tax for you. Working out if a dividend is franked is fairly easy. Wherever you see financial data on a company (such as your broker's website or <www.asx.com.au>) there is usually a column that shows what percentage of the dividends are franked.

The bad (and the ugly):

§ *Volatility.* Just like your boss's PA, shares can be oh-so-moody. Sometimes they're up, sometimes they're down and in the short term it's pretty tricky to predict which one it's going to be.

§ *You're on your own.* When you invest directly in shares, you're on your own when it comes to researching and monitoring their progress. This differs from investing in a managed fund that's looked after by a professional. You can get help from a broker (if you choose one that also gives advice), but if they work on a commission basis they may not have too much time to dedicate to you unless you're investing six figures and beyond.

§ *It takes time to research the companies in which you invest.* If you're new to the sharemarket game, it can take time at the beginning to learn how to decipher financial figures and research quality companies.

Prefer a fling to a long-term thing?

When we talk about investing in shares, we're talking about investing in the sharemarket over the long term — that is, buying and holding shares for more than five years. However, there's another way of going about it too: the fast, glamorous side of the sharemarket that you see portrayed on TV and in the movies. With know-how and plenty of research behind you, investing over the short term (or 'trading', as it's known) is also a viable investment option.

The rules for trading are quite different to investing for the long term: you buy and sell much more frequently, you look for different qualities in shares and you need to be on the ball listening out for anything that could affect your share price (such as takeovers and company announcements) — then respond accordingly. On the other hand, when you invest for the long-term you don't need to be worried about short-term fluctuations.

If you're interested in learning more about trading you should pick up a copy of Tracey Edwards's great share book, *Shopping for Shares* (Wrightbooks, 2006). She outlines both long-term and short-term share investing in a really easy to read manner.

Buying and selling shares: the aim of the game

For some, the aim of investing in shares over the long term is to make more money than they would in a bank account; for others, it might be to retire in Majorca (like lucky Laura). How much risk and return you want to live with, and the strategy you undertake to achieve this, will be unique to your situation and will largely depend on your goals.

For example, if you're young, you may decide to invest a portion of your money in quality shares with a goal to eventually sell them five or more years down the track and use the money for a deposit on a house. Or perhaps you're a little older and would like to invest in shares that pay high dividends so you can supplement your income. Have a look at the example of our ficticious friend Fran (overleaf).

Remember that one of the most important investment strategies is diversification. This means you should aim to buy a number of different types of shares across different sectors. There are all sorts of theories about how many shares you need to create a successful portfolio, but the key is to buy into enough different sectors to reduce your overall risk (but not so many that you can't keep track of them!).

Ideal portfolio

ASIC says that successful investors own shares in about eight to 14 different industries across the economy.

Example: Fictitious Fran

Fran had been saving for a few years to invest. By 2003, she had around $12500 in her bank account but was unsure what to do with her money. She started reading about shares and thought she would dip her toe in the water, using an online broker to invest in five different types of blue chip companies that were all in the S&P/ASX 100.

Fran didn't pay too much attention over the next five or so years (except when the dividends hit her bank account), but at the end of 2009 she decided to tally all her figures up to see how her investment had fared. She was surprised to find the results in the table below.

Company	No. shares bought	Share price 1 Jan 2003 ($)	2003 value of invest-ment ($)	Share price 31 Dec 2009 ($)	2009 value of invest-ment ($)	Profit (capital gain) $	Dividend income 2003–2009 $
CBA	92	27.00	2484.00	54.85	5046.20	2562.20	1323.88
Qantas	652	3.83	2497.16	2.99	1949.48	-547.68	906.28
Rio Tinto	73	33.95	2478.35	74.89	5466.97	2988.62	703.79
Wesfarmers	93	26.60	2473.80	31.27	2908.11	434.31	1113.21
Woodside	201	12.38	2488.38	47.20	9487.20	6998.82	1324.59
Totals			12421.69		24857.96	12436.27	5371.75

Value of investment in 2003: $12421.69

Value of investment in 2009: $24857.96

Capital gain: $12436.27

Dividends: $5371.75

Total profit: $17508.02
(taking into account $30 each for five brokerage fees).

Fran learned that even though some shares had done better than others her investment had more or less doubled and she'd also received thousands of dollars in dividends.

A 10-shares spread is a good ballpark figure to try and aim for. Of course, when you're starting out you can't do this all at once — just start by buying them one at a time, learning as much as you can while you go. For example you could start by saving $5000, then buy a parcel of shares worth $2500 in two companies in different sectors. Then, the next time you save $2500, you could invest in another company and so on until you feel you are adequately diversified but not drowning in annual reports. Never fear, you can always get professional help — we'll talk about this a little later.

Listed investment companies

If the thought of investing in more than two companies is sending your head spinning, you could consider investing in a listed investment company (LIC). These are companies on the ASX who invest in a spread of companies across the sharemarket themselves. By investing in them, you are in effect investing across the sharemarket. There are more than 30 LICs listed on the ASX—two of the largest are Argo Investments and the Australian Foundation Investment Company.

The deal with brokers

There are a few different ways to purchase shares, including directly via a financial adviser (if they have stockbroking qualifications) or indirectly via a managed fund.

The most common way to buy shares directly is through a stockbroker. There are around 100 firms licensed to trade on the ASX, broadly divided into two categories: advisory brokers and non-advisory brokers — each is discussed below.

Advisory or 'full service' brokers offer advice and consultation for a price and will have access to research and data. They usually charge a commission of 2.5 to 3 per cent for share trades, often with a minimum fee of around $100. Full service brokers are good if you want advice or if you have a large amount of cash to invest, but if you're investing less than $10 000 you may not get much ongoing advice if they're being paid on commission. It really comes down to what sort of research and attention you feel you need and whether it's worth the extra brokerage costs.

Most non-advisory brokers now fall under the category of 'online brokers' although there are still some brokers who'll trade for you over the phone. Online brokers are much cheaper — their fees start at $15 per trade and up to $50 for the more expensive providers — and there's generally no cost to open an account. The downside is that you'll have to do your own research (although you will get access to reports and information online, to varying degrees).

Psst ...

Finding a broker

Check out the 'Find a broker' service on the ASX website at <www.asx.com.au>. You'll find a list of questions to ask your potential broker on the Australian Securities and Investments Commission's consumer website, FIDO: <www.fido.gov.au>.

Getting started

One of the great things about shares is that you don't need much money to get started — you can buy a parcel of shares for $500 (although the ASX recommends a minimum of $2000).

You'll need to set up an account with a broker, who will require the completion of some paperwork — it's more or less as simple as opening a bank account. Some brokers like you to open a special bank account that you transfer your investment money to and from, but many will let you use your everyday transaction account.

Once you've signed up to a broker, buying shares is remarkably simple — almost as easy as transferring money from your bank account to pay a bill. You can buy shares on any ASX trading day (generally any business day between 10am and 4pm). Your order is entered into a computerised trading system called the Integrated Trading System (ITS), and then a trade occurs whenever a buy order is matched with a sell order. Bingo! It then takes around three ASX business days for the trade to be processed.

Daily trading activity

According to the ASX, Australia's average daily trading activity is more than 420 000 trades, worth over A$4.45 billion.

When is the right time to buy and sell?

The questions of when to buy and sell your shares are as old as the stock market itself, and we're afraid there is no easy answer to either one. However we do have a few ideas to help you.

'When should I buy?', you might be asking yourself. There are tons of books out there citing formulas and criteria for working out 'a good price' for a share. However, if you're investing for the long-term, the best time to buy shares may be as simple as when you know which company you want to invest in and you have the money. Remember the finance saying: 'It's time in the market, not timing the market that counts'. If you wait for the market to fall, you might be waiting too long and lose your investment mojo — that is, your motivation to invest. To time the market successfully takes skill and a good deal of luck, and even professionals often get it wrong.

Psst ...

Earnings per share (EPS) × 16

If you want to try to pick shares that are undervalued and bag a bargain, you could consider using some of the techniques that wily investors have used successfully. Benjamin Graham, a revered American investor, uses 'earnings per share' (EPS) to determine a share's intrinsic value. You can find the EPS in the business pages of the newspaper (sometimes abbreviated to 'Earn Share') or on a company's annual report. Tracey Edwards (Aussie author of *Shopping for Shares*) suggests that a share is good value when it's less than 16 times the EPS. Just multiply the figure (usually in cents) by 16 and compare it to the share price. If it's less than the share price, then it could be the right time to buy. Keep in mind that this is only one of many theories and considerations when calculating a good share price. Be sure to read widely and learn as many different techniques as possible if bargain hunting is your style.

Another tricky question to which there's no right answer is, 'When should I sell?' The best time to sell might be when you've reached your goal, or when the company itself has changed and you no longer see it being profitable into the future. It's easy to panic if your share price plunges, and it's easy to get excited if it goes up dramatically. Just remember to keep a cool head and ask yourself what your goals are, and then consider whether the company is still a quality investment. For example, if your goal is to invest for long-term wealth and the company still meets all your criteria of a good investment, you may be best to hold on to it.

Other terms that you should be aware of

There are a number of financial terms that you will undoubtedly come across as you learn more about the sharemarket. We've provided definitions for some of the most common ones you'll hear bandied about:

$ *Primary and secondary markets.* Shares in a company are sold in two ways. The first is when a company 'floats' or goes public (this event is called an IPO — an initial public offering) offering new shares to the public at a set price. This is known as buying on the primary market. The second is to buy shares on the secondary market — in this case you're buying shares that have already been issued and are now trading on the sharemarket.

$ *Market price versus at limit.* Typically, when you place an order to buy or sell shares with a broker, you can choose to place your order 'at market' (that is, you accept the going rate at the time) or 'at limit' (this is when you list the highest price you're prepared to pay or the lowest price at which you're prepared to sell).

$ *Australian Securities and Investments Commission (ASIC).* The Australian Securities and Investments Commission is Australia's corporate, markets and financial services regulator. Its role is to ensure Australia's financial markets are fair and transparent and that companies comply with their legal obligations.

$ *Wall Street.* Remember Gordon Gekko? *Wall Street* is that classic '80s movie starring Michael Douglas (as Mr 'Lunch is for wimps' Gekko) and Charlie Sheen about a young stockbroker who gets a taste of the high life, Wall Street style. It's a fascinating insight into the world of insider trading. The real Wall Street, however, refers to a tiny little street in the financial district of New York with a very big reputation. The area around the street houses the New York Stock Exchange and many of the large global investment banks and is considered the centre of the finance world.

The underworld of insider trading

Insider trading has been around for as long as the sharemarket itself and is a very dodgy (read: illegal) practice. It occurs when someone uses confidential information about a company that might affect the company's share price to buy or sell shares before the market has been informed.

Presenting case study number one: Martha Stewart. Once known in the US for her wholesomeness and homemaker tips, she made the news for all the wrong reasons in 2001 when she was found guilty of insider trading. Seems she owned thousands of shares in a company called ImClone and, on a tip from her broker (who knew of a crucial pending announcement about the company), Martha sold her shares, making a nifty profit the day before the big announcement and a plummeting share price. Both Martha and her broker were found guilty of insider trading and she was sentenced to five months in prison and fined $30 000.

If you are found guilty of insider trading in Australia you could be fined up to $500 000 and face up to 10 years imprisonment. Moral of the story: do not do this, even if you get the chance.

The greatest investor of our time: our Wazza

While some may swoon at the memory of Colin Firth (aka Mr Darcy) striding out of the lake in the BBC's *Pride and Prejudice*, it's the mind of Warren Buffett that brings a flutter to our hearts. Sure, he's an 80-year-old from Nebraska, but boy does he know how to invest.

In 2010 he was listed by *Forbes Magazine* as the third richest man in the world with an estimated net worth of US$47 billion. His company, Berkshire Hathaway (of which he is the primary shareholder and CEO) is legendary, having returned around 434 000 per cent (yes, that's right, 434 *thousand* per cent!) to its shareholders since 1965. No one-hit-wonder, Buffett is touted as one of the great investors of our time.

The great thing about Wazza (apart from his one liners — see below) is that, apart from being something of a financial genius, he speaks and writes like your wily old grandpa. He also lives a modest lifestyle and has pledged to give most of his money away to charitable organisations. According to his ex-daughter-in-law, who's written a book about his methods entitled *Buffettology* (Fireside, 1997), Buffett doesn't care about how the sharemarket as a whole is performing at all. On the contrary, he acts as if it doesn't exist and doesn't listen to tips. The only thing he focuses on is the businesses he invests in.

The moral of the story is: if you're going to learn from anyone about investing in shares, don't let it be from the guy at the dinner party you went to last week; learn from the financial woman's crumpet, Warren Buffett.

Wazza's advice

For advice straight from the horse's mouth, visit Mr Buffett's online home <www.berkshirehathaway.com> and have a read of his investment letters dating back to 1977. It's a pretty daggy-looking site but sift through the letters and you'll discover great one-liners and golden advice. It's definitely required reading for serious investors. Some of our favourites are:

→ On what to look for in a company: 'I look for companies that have (a) a business that we understand; (b) favourable long-term economics; (c) able and trustworthy management and (d) a sensible price tag' (2007).

→ On advisers: 'Beware the glib helper who fills your head with fantasies while he fills his pocket with fees' (2007).

→ On taking risk: 'When forced to choose, I will not trade even a night's sleep for the chance of extra profits' (2008).

→ On dodgy home loan lending practices: 'You only learn who has been swimming naked when the tide goes out' (2007).

The big six: what to look for when investing in shares

If you've saved up your cash, got yourself a strategy and found yourself a broker, it's time to work out which companies to invest in. Here are some great resources you can use to start your research:

$ *Company websites.* Most listed companies have an investor relations section on their website where you can access key corporate information such as annual reports, investor presentations and announcements and financial documents that can help you decide whether or not you want to buy their shares. They also have dedicated investor relations teams that you can contact to ask questions.

$ *Your broker.* Once you've signed up with a broker you'll be able to access company research and reports (to varying degrees, depending on the type of broker you use). Keep an eye out for 'wrap sheets', which are a one-page summary of useful financial information that are generally updated each weekday. Many brokers send out regular newsletters that are useful to read for information and tips.

$ Top Stocks *by Martin Roth* (Wrightbooks, published annually). If you're the sort of person who crams for exams by reading cheat notes, get your hands on a copy of the latest edition of this book. Roth publishes his pick of 100 or so Australian companies and includes a brilliant summary on each with all of the information you're ever likely to need.

$ *Yahoo finance: <www.yahoo.com.au/finance>.* This is a great website that will give you a good summary of lots of the financial information you might need. Just do a search on the company you're researching. The 'key statistics' and 'earnings summary' sections are particularly helpful.

$ *The Australian Securities Exchange.* The ASX website <www. asx.com.au> has a great research and education section.

ʃ   *Finance news.* Start to familiarise yourself with the finance sections of the newspaper or radio programs (often on the ABC). They can be hard going at first, but persevere and you'll find yourself picking up information before you know it. They often have top share picks articles, which are a good starting point for your research.

Share codes

Each company listed on the ASX is identified by a three-letter share code. For example, the share code for Westpac is WBC and the code for Woolworths is WOW. To research company information on websites such as the Australian Securities Exchange or your broker's website you'll need to enter this code. These websites also offer a facility to look up a company's code.

Psst ...

ASX Investor Education

The education section of the ASX website <www.asx.com.au> has useful tutorials you can take to learn more about shares and what to look for when researching companies. There is also a sharemarket game where you can run a dummy trial investing in shares.

In search of the perfect company

You'll need to assemble a shortlist of potential companies and research them thoroughly before you take the plunge and hand over your cash. Here are six questions to ask to help you on your way:

1   *What sort of company do you want to invest in?* It's worth thinking about whether a company's mission and ethics match your own. For example, you might think twice

before investing in any company that mines and sells uranium if you're opposed to the development of nuclear power. Asking yourself what industries or companies you *don't* want to be a part of might be a good starting point to narrow your choices down. For more information about ethical investing, have a look at chapter 9.

2   *What businesses do you know and understand?* There's a well-known piece of investment advice you'll probably hear used quite often: only invest in what you know. A good way to begin is by thinking about companies you're familiar with. Which are the companies that seem to be the best in their field? What are the services that people can't do without? Who seems to have little competition? For example, say you get your internet provided by a company who you think offers a fantastic and unique service, and that doesn't have much competition in the market. You could consider adding this to a shortlist of companies you are interested in researching further.

3   *Who is the best at their game?* If you're investing for the long term, you'll generally want to invest in quality businesses that are at the top of their game — market leaders, so to speak. If you know what type of company you want to invest in (a bank, for example), you could begin by looking at the market leaders in that area. Start by scouring for companies listed in Martin Roth's *Top Stocks*, or alternatively look through the *S&P/ASX 50* companies (the largest 50 companies in Australia) by searching for *S&P/ASX 50* on the ASX website <www.asx.com.au>.

4   *Who has done well in the past and looks to do well in the future?* Remember, profit is the aim of the game. The company you invest in should have performed consistently well over a long period of time. One of the indicators you can use to measure and compare performance is return on equity (ROE), or shareholder return. Check out a company's ROE for the past five years.

It's commonly cited that Warren Buffett often looks for a company that has an ROE of 15 per cent or more over a three-year time frame, although many profitable companies do not have an ROE as high as this. Also, consider whether or not the service the company provides has the potential for more growth in the future (that is, it's unlikely to become outdated or redundant).

> **Huh?**
>
> **Blue chip shares**
>
> The term 'blue chip shares' generally refers to shares of large companies that have a long history of sustained earnings and dividend payments. Examples include BHP Billiton, Wesfarmers and the major banks.

5   *Does the company issue dividends (and if so, how are they taxed)?* If you're investing in shares to provide you with an income stream from dividends, have a look at how much a particular share may have distributed in dividends previously. Dividend yield is generally expressed as a percentage of a share's trading price (like interest). A typical dividend payment is around 5 per cent per year. Remember, you may have to pay tax on any dividends you receive depending on whether they are franked (and your marginal tax rate). Also keep in mind that it's not a requirement for companies to issue dividends. Some do, but others reinvest their profits back into the company, which can also be a good thing for shareholders in the long run.

6   *Is the business up to its eyeballs in debt?* While some debt is okay ('borrow money to make money' and all that) lots of debt is bad and has brought many a company unstuck. Take ABC Learning for example, which went into receivership in 2008 largely due to its $1.6 billion debt. Debt is usually referred to as a percentage that represents the amount of debt a company has in relation to the amount of equity it has — otherwise called the 'debt to equity ratio'. Experts often look for a company that

generally has no more than around 50 per cent of debt compared to equity, over a period of time (unless there's a good reason for a higher debt level, such as the company has undergone a recent takeover, for example).

Virginia's story (age 70)

When I was young, the 1929 crash was still clearly etched in people's memories. While many people feared the stock market because of the crash, others were boasting about the money they made trading shares. I became interested and started listening regularly to ABC radio in the 1980s when I was in my 40s, as it broadcast the prices of all shares each day and also had a Saturday morning financial advice show I enjoyed. My curiosity led me to go to the old stock exchange and see how it worked. I attended free lectures and open days held by the Australian Securities Exchange.

I first started investing six years later with small parcels of shares, which I sold if they made a reasonable profit. I then bought larger parcels in IPO (new share) floats such as Commonwealth Bank, Bank of Melbourne and Woolworths, which became profitable purchases. I kept reinvesting my dividends and increased my share holdings when I could.

One of the biggest hurdles I had to overcome was the fear of losing my money. However, despite this fear, I made good capital gains on many of the companies I bought. Along the way I have learnt many things: firstly, that mass hysteria can make a market fall unexpectedly. I've learnt not to buy companies with high borrowings and gearing. I've also learnt that some journalists have a vested interested in talking up companies. I'm sceptical of advice from some broking firms as well.

The advice I would give other women is to try to find companies that have a unique but necessary business with little competition, then read as many books as they can find to educate themselves about the workings of the market. Finally, as it takes time to make money, investing into a product that returns dividends, interest or capital gains from a young age should ensure you'll be better off in later life.

Checklist: getting ready to buy shares

If the thought of investing in the sharemarket appeals, here are some simple steps that will help get you on your way to becoming a sharemarket guru.

1   *Educate yourself.* Go to the Australian Securities Exchange website <www.asx.com.au> and check out some of the online courses in the education section. Download the *Getting Started in Shares* booklet and take some of the lessons in the teacher resources section. Pick up an easy-to-read book about investing in shares. Start to open your eyes to the finance news — read the business section and finance supplements in the newspapers. Talk to people you know who've successfully invested in shares and find out how they go about it.

2   *Put together a plan.* Work out how shares fit in with your overall financial goals. This will determine how much you initially invest, how often you'll buy parcels of shares and how many different types of shares you invest in. Seek financial advice from an accountant or a financial adviser if you need assistance developing a sound investment strategy that ensures your investments are adequately diversified. Also, consider the tax implications of your investment.

      Save up for your first parcel of shares. You can start from as little as $500, but $5000 is a much better figure to begin with. If you need help with budgeting and saving go back and re-read chapters 2 and 3.

3   *Find a broker.* Decide what type of broker you'd like (full service or online) and look around for the best deal for you. The ASX website has an up-to-date list of online brokers. Publications such as *Money* magazine (published monthly by ACP Magazines) often list the best value brokers so keep your eyes peeled. You'll have to fill out an application form and send them a copy of your ID but it's really as simple as opening a bank account.

4   *Work out which companies you want to invest in.* Create
     a shortlist of companies by asking questions such as:
     are they a market leader? Do they have much debt?
     Have they historically made good returns over a long
     period? What dividends have they paid in the past? You
     can source this sort of information from *Top Stocks* by
     Martin Roth (published annually by Wrightbooks), from
     annual reports or from your broker. Most finance books
     specialising in shares have a long list of criteria used for
     selecting shares that you could look at too. After you've
     answered these questions you should be ready to pick a
     company or two (or three) in which to start investing.
     Work out what price you're willing to pay for the shares.
     Most finance books about shares give advice on how to
     evaluate a good share price.

5   *Buy your shares and track them!* Here comes the easy part:
     buy your shares through your broker. You'll be surprised
     at how simple it is. Keep track of your paperwork and read
     the annual reports. Check your investment regularly and
     compare it with benchmark indexes. For example, if you
     bought shares in BHP Billiton, you could compare their
     annual return with that of a resources index. Remember to
     keep the big picture in mind. Shares go up and down — if
     your share price is fluctuating but the index or the share
     prices of other companies in the same industry are
     fluctuating too, it's most likely to be a reflection on the
     market as a whole.

Remember: always ask for help if you need it

If you don't feel confident going through the whole process alone,
you should seek help from a full-service broker, or alternatively
an accountant or a licensed financial adviser. We tell you where
you can find them in the 'Help when you need it' section at the
back of the book.

managed funds

There once was a girl called Celeste
Who said 'Hmm...I'd like to invest!'
She thought shares were for her
But found choosing them 'errgh'
So a managed fund suited her best.

If the idea of investing in the sharemarket appeals to you, but you don't feel confident enough to do it on your own, never fear — managed funds might be the option you've been looking for.

In a nutshell, a managed fund lets you combine your money with other people's, and have a professional manage your money for you and do the investing. The great thing about managed funds is that you don't need much money to start with, yet you still get exposure to a wide range of investment options including cash, property and shares — something you'd find impossible to do on your own without a lot of cash. It's a bit like pitching in with a bunch of mates for a friend's birthday present—it's the only way you're going to be able to afford that really great gift. By paying professional fund managers to do the work for you, you're putting your money in the hands of experts—so you can leave the day-to-day stress of managing your investment to them. It's hard to put a price on that! In this chapter we'll cover:

ς managed funds 101: exactly what are managed funds?

ς types of managed funds: single-sector versus multi-sector

ς the big five: what to look for when choosing a managed fund

ς checklist: how to go about investing in a managed fund.

At a glance

Here's a snapshot of six things you might like to know about investing in managed funds:

→ **Who is best suited to investing in managed funds?** Beginner investors, the time-poor or those who just prefer to leave it to the experts.

→ **How much money do I need to start?** It varies, but lots of funds let you buy in from as little as $1000 if you also sign up to a regular savings plan.

→ **How much can I expect to make?** It depends on the type of fund you invest in and the amount of risk you're prepared to take, but here's an example: according to the Australian Securities and Investments Commission (ASIC), $10 000 invested in a balanced managed fund with a mix of investments (including shares, listed property, cash and fixed interest) can be expected to return around 8 per cent per annum over the long term and will be worth around $14 700 after five years (not taking inflation into account).

Alternatively, if you invested your $10 000 in an aggressive growth fund, you could expect to earn an average of 11.5 per cent per annum over the long term, which would bring your investment to around $17 234 after five years.

→ **What kind of time frame works best for managed funds?**
A minimum of three to seven years, depending on the type of fund. If you're investing in a conservative type of fund (for example, one that invests primarily in cash) you should aim to invest for a minimum of three years. If you're investing in a more aggressive type of fund (one that invests primarily in shares, for example) you should aim to invest for a minimum of seven years to account for any sharemarket volatility.

→ **How much work goes into investing in managed funds?**
Managed funds are low maintenance. Most of the work comes at the start when you're researching to find a fund.

→ **Look out for:** fees charged by the fund manager. Remember, you'll also have to pay tax on any money your fund makes.

Managed funds 101: exactly what are managed funds?

Also called 'unit trusts' or 'managed investment schemes', managed funds were introduced in Australia in the 1930s and there are now a ridiculously confusing number to choose from, each with different objectives and results. Managed funds are run either by large financial institutions such as banks or by smaller specialist management firms. Each fund is headed up by a fund manager, who is responsible for investing the money you put into the fund. He or she will do this in accordance with the fund's objectives and may invest in cash, property or shares — or a mixture of these.

Managed funds have lots of admirers

According to the ABS, more than 9 million Australians in 2009 invested in managed funds to the value of $1.2 trillion. This makes investing in managed funds an extremely popular type of investment.

The aim of the game

When you invest in a managed fund, the fund manager pools your money with other people's and divides the total investment into units of equal value. How many units you get depends on their price at the time you buy, and how much cash you invest. For example, if you invest $1000 in a managed fund on a day when the unit price is at $1, you will have bought 1000 units in the fund. When the unit price rises or falls, so does the value of your investment.

The unit price will fluctuate from day to day depending on the market value, but the aim of the game is for the value of your units to increase over time so you can ultimately sell them for a tidy profit. You may also receive regular interest or dividends if the fund's assets generate earnings. You can choose to take these dividends as a payout (hello new dress) or in units reinvested into your account (hello future riches).

To market, to market, to buy a fat pig

Lots of fund managers will let you start investing with as little as $1000, but often with the proviso that you also sign up to a regular savings plan where you make monthly contributions (usually a minimum of $100) via direct debit straight from your transaction account—a brilliant, pain-free way of building up your savings over time. Have a look at figures 6.1 and 6.2 to remind yourself of the amazing effect that compound interest can have on an investment over time.

Example 1: compound interest over 10 years

Let's say you start by investing $2000, and make monthly payments of $200 for the next 10 years, reinvesting any income you receive and earning eight per cent growth (a reasonable annual return to expect on a balanced managed fund), which compounds annually. How much do you think you'd have after 10 years? Check out figure 6.1 for the answer.

Figure 6.1: compound interest — monthly contributions of $200 over 10 years

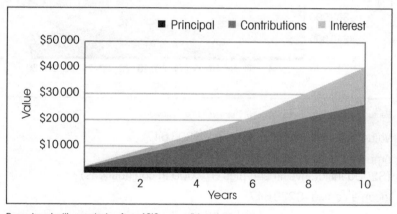

Reproduced with permission from ASIC <www.fido.asic.gov.au>.

Value of investment after 10 years: $40574

Amount invested: $26000
($2000 initial investment, plus $24000 in contributions)
Income earned: $14574

Example 2: compound interest over 30 years

Now, let's look at what happens if you continue to contribute $200 as per example 1, for a further 20 years. The results, shown in figure 6.2 (overleaf), are quite amazing.

Figure 6.2: compound interest — monthly contributions of $200 over 30 years

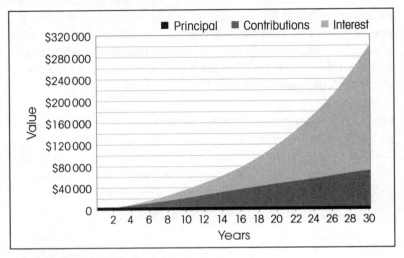

Reproduced with permission from ASIC <www.fido.asic.gov.au>.

Value of investment after 30 years: $303 647

Amount invested: $74 000
($2000 initial investment, plus $72 000 in contributions)

Income earned: $229 647

Nothing like a compound interest chart to make you feel inspired, huh? While these charts are fairly simplistic and don't take into account the less glamorous side of things — such as fees (more about these in a moment), tax or inflation — they are an excellent example of how compound interest really does make your investment add up over time.

Another great thing about managed funds: they have a high level of liquidity compared with an investment such as residential property, for example, which may take months to sell. You can sell your units whenever you want, and you should receive your money within a week (or two weeks if you invest in a share fund).

Psst ...

FIDO

The ASIC consumer website, FIDO <www.fido.gov.au>, has lots of helpful information about managed funds, including a calculator that helps you work out the effects of different investment options, fees, making regular contributions and changing funds over time.

Fees: what to look out for

Just like that pesky mosquito you hear buzzing around your head at night when you go camping, fees are annoying and here to stay (however we'll show you how you can minimise them in a minute). The main kinds of fees you need to watch out for are:

$ *Entry fees.* These typically range from 0 to 5 per cent of any money you invest in the fund, depending on the investment. Entry fees are usually deducted from your balance. Note that a percentage of this entry fee will often be paid to your financial adviser (if you have one) as a commission.

$ *Ongoing management fees.* Often called an MER (Management Expense Ratio), ongoing management fees are generally between 0.5 and 3 per cent of your total investment.

$ *Exit fees.* Not all funds charge exit fees, but many do. Exit fees can range from 0 to 2 per cent of the value of any units you sell.

$ *Performance fees.* Some managed funds also charge performance fees if the fund does particularly well, however this is not very common.

The amount you pay in fees will have a big impact on how large your fund balance grows. So if you decide to invest in a managed fund make sure you take this into account.

For example, say you invested $10 000 in two managed funds — both were completely equal in every respect, and with each earning 8 per cent per annum. The only difference is that one charges an MER of 0.8 per cent and the other charges an MER of 2.5 per cent. Take a look at figure 6.3 to see how the results might pan out after 10 years.

Figure 6.3: the effect of fees on the growth of managed funds over 10 years

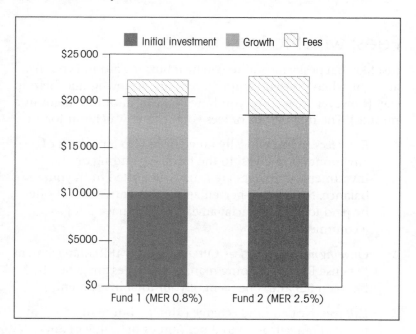

Managed Fund 1: MER: 0.8 per cent

Value of investment after 10 years: $20 539

Total fees paid: $1714

Managed Fund 2: MER: 2.5 per cent

Value of investment after 10 years: $18 310

Total fees paid: $4293

As you see, no matter how small the fees might seem, they really can make a difference over time. If you choose a fund that charges higher management fees, you should be confident (based on its historical performance and rating) that the fund is likely to bring in high returns to compensate for this.

The good, the bad and the ugly

Here are some pluses and minuses to consider when investing in managed funds.

The good:

ß   *You can start with a little.* You don't need much money to start with and many fund managers will let you make monthly contributions if you choose, which makes regular saving nice and hassle-free.

ß   *Diversification.* You can invest in a range of investments that might be well beyond your reach as an individual investor — a fund can invest in cash, property, Australian shares, international shares or any mixture of these. Share funds can hold anything from a few to 50 or more stocks.

ß   *Expert management.* A team of investment professionals with lots of experience and information at their fingertips will be making the day-to-day decisions about what to do with the fund's money and by law must use due diligence to manage your fund effectively.

The bad (and the ugly):

ß   *Fees.* The fees charged can really add up over time and take a chunk of your investment compared to, say, investing in shares directly, where one-off brokerage fees can be relatively small. Fund managers typically charge a mix of entry fees, ongoing management fees and exit fees, but they vary tremendously.

$ *Lack of control.* Investing in a managed fund takes away your say over where your money is invested. While you can choose a fund based on asset class, you won't have any choice in where your money is invested after that. For example, if you invest in a share fund you're investing your money in shares of companies that the manager selects, not you. And if you invest in a fund that's heavily weighted towards shares, your investment will be affected by sharemarket volatility. Such managed funds would be better seen as long-term investments rather than short-term ones.

$ *Not-so-expert management.* Your investment is only going to do as well as the team who invests it. If the people who manage your fund are not as great as you'd hoped, or if there is a change in personnel and the new managers aren't so good, the value of your units might decrease. Of course, it's unlikely to be a huge issue if you choose a reputable financial institution — more about how to tackle that one later.

Types of managed funds: single-sector versus multi-sector

Picking the right managed fund can be as overwhelming as trying to navigate your way through an Ikea store on a Saturday morning. There are more than 10 000 funds on offer in Australia, and it can be hard to know where to start. The best way to narrow down your search is to work out which type of fund you're looking for. Fund types are generally categorised as either single-sector funds or multi-sector funds and here's a bit about both.

Single-sector funds

Single-sector funds invest in a single asset class (that is, one area of investment). The types of asset classes that single sector funds may specialise in are generally defined as:

$ cash

$ fixed interest securities (such as government bonds)

$ property (not the white-picket-fence kind but the commercial kind, traded on stock exchanges)

$ Australian shares

$ international shares.

Keep in mind that even if you choose to invest in a single-sector fund, it's still possible that you'll be diversifying your investment. For example, if you choose an Australian share fund, you may be investing in companies in industries as diverse as mining, finance and retail.

Multi-sector funds

Also known as diversified funds, multi-sector funds invest across a range of asset classes. They are usually defined as one of three categories: conservative or defensive; balanced; or growth. We'll now discuss each category of multi-sector fund with reference to its risks and returns and the recommended time frame for investment.

Conservative or defensive

These funds usually hold most of their money in low-risk assets such as cash and fixed interest and a small percentage in higher-risk growth assets such as Australian and international shares and property. Here are some facts about conservative or defensive funds:

$ *Risk and return*: low returns and low risk. In other words, you're likely to make less money from a conservative fund than a growth fund, but it's a more secure investment because it's primarily invested in fixed-interest investments (such as cash) and therefore not subject to fluctuations on the sharemarket.

§   *Time frame*: think about investing for around three years. These funds are good for investors looking for a reasonably secure place to park their money for a relatively short period of time.

Figure 6.4 shows an example of the makeup of a conservative or defensive fund.

Figure 6.4: example of a conservative or defensive fund

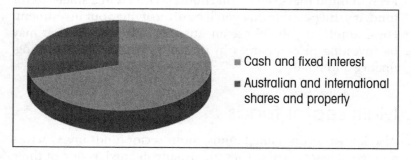

■ Cash and fixed interest
■ Australian and international shares and property

Balanced

These funds usually hold around half of their money in low-risk assets such as cash and fixed interest, and half in growth assets such as Australian and international shares and property. Here are some facts about balanced funds:

§   *Risk and return*: low to moderate risk. Because balanced funds hold a greater percentage of their assets in property and shares, you can expect a higher return for your money than if you invested in a conservative fund. However, these funds will experience greater volatility because they're more likely to be subject to sharemarket fluctuations.

§   *Time frame*: aim to invest for a minimum of four to five years. This will give you a chance to ride out any fluctuations in the sharemarket.

Figure 6.5 shows an example of the makeup of a balanced fund.

Figure 6.5: example of a balanced fund

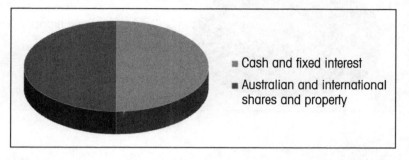

Growth

Growth funds go for gold and usually hold most of their assets in Australian or international shares (or a mixture of both) with a small percentage in property or fixed interest. Here are some facts about growth funds:

$ *Risk and return*: strong capital growth and a higher risk. You've got the best chance of making high returns with a growth fund, but this stronger growth comes with more risk as the sharemarket can be volatile, particularly in the short term. (Remember that over the long term, Australian and international shares have made the highest returns).

$ *Time frame*: aim to invest for a minimum of around five to seven years — that way you should have invested for long enough to achieve good capital growth and to ride out any sharemarket fluctuation.

Figure 6.6 (overleaf) shows an example of the makeup of a growth fund.

Figure 6.6: example of a growth fund

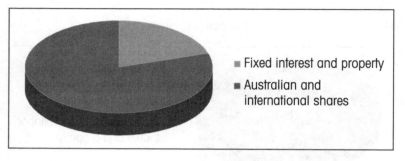

- Fixed interest and property
- Australian and international shares

Vanessa's story (age 31)

I was utterly disinterested in finance until my mid 20s. It wasn't that I was bad with money—I didn't have any debt or anything. It's just that it was never part of any consideration in my life; I found it boring and irrelevant.

But after a break-up with a boyfriend, and a fateful conversation with a friend who was a very savvy investor, my whole outlook on finance changed. I realised that I needed to take control of my financial future in order to be independent and be able to do the things that I wanted with my life, such as travelling and working in a job I loved in the arts that would never pay me very well.

I really didn't know where to start, so I bought some finance books and dedicated myself to learning. I wanted to find an easy, low-maintenance way of investing that wouldn't require much cash to start with. So I decided upon managed funds as my first investment—it seemed an easy way to invest in a number of different companies and give me the diversification I had learnt an investor should have. I also liked the fact that I could contribute regular amounts from my bank account easily each month.

Getting started was hard in the beginning; I was overwhelmed by the sheer choice of funds, but once I narrowed it down to tax-effective Australian share funds, my research became much easier. I remember feeling quite nervous sending off my form and depositing my first $3000 — but since then I haven't looked back. I still make regular monthly automatic payments and although the price of my units has fluctuated, I'm confident that over the long term it's a good investment.

I'm much more confident now and have since made other investments, but I would still recommend managed funds to first-time investors. However, I would issue a strong word of warning about the fees: they really can add up over time, so make sure you understand how much you're paying and check that it isn't substantially more than the fees charged by similar funds. Index funds are great as they are low in fees. If you're worried about the performance of your fund, I'd recommend comparing your results with those of similar funds (comparing apples with apples and all that).

Other terms that you should be aware of

By this stage, all the technical jargon might be tempting you to give up and start reading *Twilight* for the fourth time, but there are a couple of things you should learn before you throw your hands up in exasperation — particularly if you go down the route of investing via a financial adviser. Here are some of the more common terms you'll come across if you do decide to invest in managed funds. Forewarned is forearmed!

Retail versus wholesale managed funds

There are essentially two kinds of managed funds: retail and wholesale.

Retail funds are the type that most people buy, and that generally come with a nice glossy information brochure full of useful information that tries to sell the fund to you. Here's a list of some of the big, well-known professional retail fund managers:

- $ Australian Ethical Investment: <www.australianethical. com.au>

- $ BT: <www.bt.com.au>

- $ Colonial First State: <www.colonialfirststate.com.au>

- $ Hunter Hall Ethical Managed Funds: <www.hunterhall.com.au>

- $ ING: <www.ing.com.au>

- $ MLC: <www.mlc.com.au>

- $ Perpetual: <www.perpetual.com.au>

- $ Platinum Asset Management: <www.platinum.com.au>.

They all offer a range of managed funds with investment options across the different asset classes.

Wholesale funds set their fees at a lower rate than retail funds, and are available to individual investors. They often require a minimum initial investment in the hundreds of thousands of dollars, so they are most often bought by big institutional investors such as banks who invest large sums of money in them. Great if you have the cash, not so great if you don't. If you're lucky enough to have the big bucks required to invest in wholesale funds, check out the following list of some of the wholesale funds in Australia:

- $ BT: <www.bt.com.au>

- $ ING: <www.ing.com.au>

- $ Perpetual: <www.perpetual.com.au>

- $ Vanguard Investments: <www.vanguard.com.au>.

You'll find that not as many fund managers offer wholesale funds as they do retail.

Mastertrusts and wrap accounts

Mastertrusts and wrap accounts are similar beasts: when you invest in either one, you're buying into an umbrella fund that lets you spread your money across lots of funds managed by different fund managers. This gives you a fantastic range of investment options. Mastertrusts and wrap accounts even let you hold and trade shares in companies on the Australian sharemarket — for example, you could buy shares in Westpac or Fosters if that takes your fancy. They're often recommended by financial advisers as a convenient way of managing your investment portfolio.

On the plus side, mastertrusts and wrap accounts give you access to both retail and wholesale funds, with some offering hundreds of different investment choices. You can easily switch between investments without paying fees — once you're in, you're in. And they offer simple and clear reporting, so it's easy to see exactly how your investments are faring.

On the minus side, mastertrusts and wrap accounts charge fees that can be very high, and this can really eat into your investment. This is because there are effectively two 'layers' of fees — the administrators of the mastertrust or wrap accounts charge their own fees and the fund managers who manage the funds offered by the mastertrust or wrap account also charge fees for managing the funds. If you don't see yourself wanting to switch your investments too often, or if you've got less than $100 000 to invest, mastertrusts and wrap accounts probably aren't for you.

Here are some of the big, well respected fund managers who offer mastertrusts and wrap accounts:

$ Asgard: <www.asgard.com.au>

$ Aviva Australia: <www.avivagroup.com.au>

$ BT: <www.bt.com.au>

$ Colonial First State: <www.colonialfirststate.com.au>.

Check out their websites for full details — you might find that you have to go through a financial adviser to invest in this type of fund.

Index funds and exchange traded funds

Index funds are a smart way of buying cash, property, and Australian or international shares via a managed fund. Index funds don't try to pick and choose among all the different shares on offer, and they don't try to outperform the market like garden-variety managed funds do. Instead, they try to match the investment performance of a given index, such as the All Ordinaries index on the sharemarket. They are sometimes called 'passively managed funds' for this reason.

The great thing about index funds is that they're much cheaper to manage than retail managed funds, which means lower fees for you. They make diversification across the Australian sharemarket easy and they are often tax-effective forms of investment because they invest in Aussie shares, which often pay franked dividends.

Managed funds and franked dividends

In case you need a little reminder, some Australian companies issue franked dividends. A franked dividend is one on which the company has already paid part or all of the company tax on it, before it heads your way. So if you've invested in a managed fund that holds Australian shares it's possible that the fund will receive franked dividends which could mean you'll pay less tax on your earnings too. Some managed funds (often referred to as imputation funds) specialise in buying Australian shares that pay franked dividends.

You might also hear about exchange traded funds (or ETFs). ETFs are a type of index fund, but they are traded like shares on the Australian Securities Exchange instead of being managed like a traditional index fund. So you'll pay a broker a brokerage fee every time you buy ETFs, rather than paying a fee to a fund manager.

If you're interested in investing in index funds or ETFs, or if you'd just like more information, check out Vanguard Investments at <www.vanguard.com.au> (Vanguard is considered a specialist index fund manager) or iShares <www.ishares.com.au>.

The big five: what to look for when choosing a managed fund

When you're shopping around for a managed fund there are a few things you'll need to keep in mind. Here are five questions you should always ask:

1   *Does the fund manager have a good reputation?* It goes without saying that you should look for a fund that's managed by an established and reputable financial institution. You wouldn't buy a new BMW from Dodgy Frank's Car Yard, so be just as careful to invest your money with a top-notch fund manager. Start by getting your hands on a copy of *Money* magazine (published by ACP Magazines) — it regularly features articles about managed funds. Jump online to check out any fund manager you might have heard about. And have a look at fund ratings by Morningstar.

Psst ...

Morningstar

Morningstar provides independent information about fund performance and awards star ratings out of five. Think hotel reviews, but for managed funds. It also lists a fund's previous one-, three- and five-year returns (where available). You can find Morningstar ratings listed at the back of each month's *Smart Investor* magazine (published by the *Australian Financial Review*), in the financial pages of the big newspapers or online at <www.morningstar.com.au>.

2   *How has the fund performed over time?* It's important that the fund you choose has a good track record. Although past performance is no guarantee of future performance, if you choose a fund that's done well over the past five years in comparison to similar funds, you're off to a good start. Keep in mind that if you're looking at a fund that invests heavily in one particular asset class (say, Australian shares) but there just happens to have been a recent slump in the Australian sharemarket none of the fund managers will appear to be performing particularly well. Don't worry — this will almost certainly turn around due to the cyclical nature of the economy. Just remember, you should always compare the results of a fund to that of similar funds — compare apples with apples, as they say.

> *Huh?*
>
> **PDS**
>
> Every managed investment has one — a brochure called a product disclosure statement (PDS). It provides detailed information about the investment, its objectives, fees and suggested time frame for investing. It also includes an application form for buying units in the fund.

3   *What are the fund's objectives?* Make sure you understand exactly what the fund is trying achieve — you'll find the objectives outlined in the product disclosure statement (PDS). Does the fund aim to beat a specialised benchmark? Is it aiming for capital growth (an increase in your unit value) or will it provide income (interest or dividends)? Does the fund invest in international or Australian shares? These are just a few examples of possible fund objectives — whatever they are, you'll need to decide if they match your own.

4   *Does the fund have a regular investment plan?* If you plan on making monthly contributions to a fund directly from your bank account you'll need to make sure that the fund you choose has a regular investment plan. It's a

great way of building up your savings over time with small amounts of money. This is called 'dollar cost averaging'.

5   *What fees does the fund charge?* Fees can take a chunk out of your investment over time. They vary widely between fund managers, so it pays to look at this carefully when you're choosing a fund. A word of warning: you're likely to pay higher fees if the fund you choose is weighted heavily towards shares, particularly international shares. Index funds are the exception to this and charge relatively low fees even though they invest in Australian shares.

Huh?

Dollar cost averaging

If you're automatically making contributions to a managed fund every month, both when the market is doing well and when it isn't, the price at which you'll be buying units in the fund will generally average out in the long run (some months the unit price will be high, other months the price will be low). This is called dollar cost averaging and can be a very good thing for the average investor because timing the market (which is tricky, even for professional investors) becomes less important.

Checklist: how to go about investing in a managed fund

If you've come this far and think that managed funds might be your cup of tea, here are some simple steps to guide you on your way to becoming a happy managed funds investor:

1   *Decide on your plan of attack.* Ask yourself how much risk you're comfortable with and decide on a time frame. Do you want to invest in a conservative fund or do you hope to achieve higher returns by investing in a growth fund?

When do you see yourself needing the money from your investment?

Save up for your initial deposit. Refer back to chapters 2 and 3 and take a refresher course on budgeting and saving if you need it. Decide whether or not you want to make regular contributions to the fund.

2   *Find the fund for you.* Work out what type of fund suits you best. For example, if you've decided to go for growth, do you want Australian shares only, or a mixture of Australian and international shares? Check out Morningstar's ratings and results over time and narrow down your choice to two or three funds. Request a PDS for each fund and have a read, taking into account fees, regular investment plan options, investment time frame and tax implications. You should be able to get a PDS from a financial adviser (if you have one), directly from the fund manager or through a discount online broker.

Psst ...

Rebates

Discount online brokers (including CommSec, E*TRADE Australia, InvestSMART and YourShare) are specialist investment brokers who don't give investment advice however will sell you whatever fund you're after—great for people who've done their own research and know exactly what fund they want to invest in. By requesting a PDS and investing through a discount online broker, the entry fee is rebated to you—a sneaky way of avoiding this fee. You could also receive a rebate of a percentage of the 'trailing commissions' (ongoing management fees) that are usually paid to financial advisers—check with the broker as their services differ. This could save you a lot of money.

3   *Invest away.* Once you decide on the fund for you, it's time
    to invest! Most people buy into managed funds either
    with the help of a financial adviser (who may be paid
    a commission) or by themselves via a discount online
    broker. If you do it yourself it's as simple as filling out the
    application form that comes with the PDS. Remember
    to make sure that the broker's company stamp is on the
    application form (usually in the adviser information
    section of the form) so the fund manager knows you're
    eligible to receive a rebate on your fees. Your fund should
    be up and running within a couple of weeks. Give yourself
    a pat on the back!

4   *Keep your eyes peeled.* Keep an eye on your fund from time
    to time to see how it's performing. (However don't do
    this too often — it could send you batty!) Most funds will
    give you access to the investor section of their website and
    will set you up with a username and password so you can
    see exactly how your units are doing whenever you want.
    Don't stress out if the value of your investment regularly
    rises and falls — that's natural.

    You should also have a look at the Morningstar
    ratings tables at the back of the *Australian Financial
    Review*'s *Smart Investor* magazine now and then to see
    how your fund is performing against similar funds. If you
    suspect your fund isn't performing up to scratch it might
    be time for you to do some investigating. If you need
    advice about this consider going to a financial adviser.

5   *Keep yourself nice.* At the risk of sounding like your mother,
    keep any paperwork and statements you receive from your
    fund — preferably in the one place. Makes it a lot easier to
    grab information if you need it and when tax time rolls
    around every year.

Tax talk

Managed funds invest in different asset classes, and each will come with its own tax implications. For example, if you're in a managed fund that's primarily invested in cash, you'll have earned interest throughout the year. This will have to be declared on your tax return. If you're in a managed fund that's heavily invested in Australian shares, you're likely to have received dividends throughout the year that will also have to be declared; you might also have received franking credits. Whatever the scenario, at the end of each financial year you'll receive a full statement from your fund manager outlining any change in the value of your investment and any other information necessary for you to fill out your tax return accurately.

Remember: always ask for help if you need it

Women aren't afraid to ask for help — whether it's with directions or otherwise! If you don't feel confident going through the whole process on your own, you should consider seeing a licensed financial adviser. We tell you where you can find one in the 'Help when you need it' section at the back of this book.

chapter 7

superannuation

There once was a woman called Joyce
Who lived a life frugal by choice
Years came and went
She saved rather than spent
And now drives to bowls in a Rolls Royce.

So, we've come to superannuation. 'Spare me', you're probably thinking. But before you skip ahead to the next chapter, bear with us for a minute.

Being unprepared for retirement is your single biggest financial risk as a woman — and unfortunately the odds are stacked against you. According to a study commissioned by AMP in November 2009, you're likely to live longer than a man; you'll also take more time out of the workforce, and earn less throughout your career. All this adds up to a future where you may not have enough savings to live off, and so become reliant on government help. Anyone living off the pension now can tell you that it's not an easy life.

It's so tempting to put off thinking about your super-annuation; retirement seems so very far away, particularly if you've only recently joined the workforce. It's also *trés* boring — let's face it, bringing up super is unlikely to set dinner party conversation alight. But if you get your super sorted out now, you could actually set yourself up financially and enjoy a retirement lived in style.

Despite the intricate laws governing superannuation in Australia, and the constant changes we hear about in the media, you only really need to understand the basics in order to get it right. That's where this chapter comes in. So dose up on caffeine, read on and find out how you could make a massive difference to your future. In this chapter we'll cover:

$ superannuation 101: what is super and how much will you need?

$ sorting out your super: how much money do you have and where is it?

$ boosting your super: ways to go about it

$ checklist: get on track for a fabulous future.

At a glance

Here's a snapshot of six things you might like to know about investing in superannuation.

→ **Who is best suited to investing in superannuation?** Everyone. Every Australian will need an income after they've retired.

→ **How much money do I need to start?** Australian employers are required by law to contribute to a super fund for every employee earning over $450 (before tax) per month. Otherwise, anyone can open up their own super fund; you usually need around $1000 to start.

→ **How much can I expect to make?** This will depend on the investment option you choose within your super fund, the fees charged by the super fund, whether you make additional contributions and the number of years until your retirement. Half a million to a million to retire on wouldn't be out of the question.

→ **What kind of time frame works best for superannuation?** Mega-long-term. You could be investing in super for 40 years or more, depending on how long you're in the workforce and how many years until your retirement. Note that you won't be able to access your super (except in extreme circumstances) until you hit retirement age (currently deemed to be 60 for anyone born after 1 July 1964).

→ **How much work goes into investing in superannuation?** Investing in superannuation is low maintenance, especially if you're investing in a super fund recommended by your employer. Otherwise, most of the work comes at the start when you're researching to find a fund.

→ **Look out for:** fees. These can vary widely between different super funds—some can be pretty steep, and this will affect your final balance. Look carefully and weigh up whether you're getting value for money.

Superannuation 101: what is super and how much will you need?

Superannuation is your retirement fund—a pool of money you build up over your working life that will provide you with an income after you've hung up your employment boots. Super was made compulsory in 1992 by the Australian Government to help address the anticipated increase in pension payments brought about by an aging population. The minimum super contribution is now set at 9 per cent of your earnings, but some industry groups argue that this just isn't enough; they suggest that a 15 per cent contribution is necessary for most people to accrue enough savings to retire on without financial hardship.

How does it work?

If you earn more than $450 before tax each month, your employer must pay a minimum of 9 per cent of your ordinary time earnings (that is, not including overtime) on top of your wage into a super fund of your choice. By law this must occur every three months. The government also gives tax breaks to people who make additional contributions to boost their super. Your savings will build up over the years and when you retire your super is paid to you as either a lump sum, an income stream (like a pension) or a combination of both.

Look into the crystal ball...

Imagine it's the year 2040. You're close to retiring, and you're not alone — around seven million Australians, or 22 per cent of the population, are now aged over 65 (back in 2010 it was only 13.5 per cent).

Unfortunately, all the predictions made decades ago have proven correct, and years of spending rather than saving have resulted in most people having insufficient money put away for retirement. By the time you retire (possibly in 2040) the average super balance of a 64-year-old woman about to retire is $200 300. For men, it's $350 900. While that amount may sound mildly respectable in 2010, after 30 years of inflation, a super balance of that size is not going to be quite so 'super', and is unlikely to support a woman for 22 years of retirement.

The scary facts

There are several reasons why, as a woman, you're up against it in the happy retirement stakes:

$ *You're likely to live longer than a man.* Today, 92 per cent of women living in Australia live until the age of 65 (compared to 87 per cent of men). Once they've reached that milestone, women can expect to live for about another 22 years (for men it's about 19 years). That's a long retirement to fund.

$ *You're likely to be paid less than your male counterparts.* Even when they work full time, women's average earnings are around 83 per cent of male earnings. As our super contributions are often linked to how much we earn, men generally finish their working lives with more in super than women, even though they can expect fewer years in retirement.

$ *You're more likely to take time out of the workforce than a man.* Women are far more likely than men to take time out from their career to raise a family or to care for others, and often only return to part-time work once their children reach school age. This kind of disruption to a woman's career can have a startling impact on her final super balance.

You can't eat your house

Super industry bodies suggest that in 2010 around $39 000 a year (after tax) as a single female or $52 000 as a couple will provide a comfortable lifestyle. In order to generate that kind of income, a single female would require a superannuation balance of around $650 000 and a couple $860 000 (in today's dollars) when they retire. For those of us retiring in the future these figures will need to be increased to take the effects of inflation into account.

It's easy to see why it's even more important for women to save for their future than men, but also why it's so much harder. In 2009 Australian women aged between 55 and 64 had an average super balance of only $60 700 (compared to $130 900 for men). While women retiring in the future won't be quite so badly off (as they'll have been in the workforce for longer while compulsory employer super contributions have been in effect) financial experts generally agree that Australians are not saving enough to afford a comfortable retirement.

Don't forget that once you've retired, you'll have time on your hands to do all those things you might not have had a chance to do while you were in the workforce, such as travelling — and that costs money. The question is, where is this money going to come from? While buying and paying off a house is a worthy achievement, it's not going to provide you with an income once you retire, so you'll need a Plan B for that — and that's superannuation.

Retirement shouldn't be a time to start watching every cent, but unfortunately that's the reality for a lot of people. That's what makes super such an important investment, and all the more reason to get your skates on to do something about it.

The good, the bad and the ugly

Here are some pluses and minuses to consider when it comes to investing in superannuation.

The good:

$ *Your money is locked away.* There's nothing like forced saving to make sure you keep your hands out of the cookie jar, and the government knows this — which is why they offer tax incentives to lock your money away for retirement.

$ *Tax.* Super is considered the golden child of tax-effective investment. Any money you salary sacrifice (take-home pay that you forgo to contribute to your super) is contributed in pre-tax dollars. This means that you won't pay tax on it at your regular marginal rate, but rather at a very reasonable 15 per cent instead. You'll also only pay up to 15 per cent tax on any interest or distributions of income your fund pays throughout the year. Once retirement rolls around, you won't pay any tax at all if you use your super as a source of income.

$ *Life insurance and death benefits.* If you're interested in taking out life insurance you can usually buy it through your super fund at a discounted rate (more about insurance in chapter 10).

The bad (and the ugly):

$ *Your money is locked away.* You can't touch it until you're around 60, which could be light-years away. In the meantime, if some other investment opportunity were to come knocking (ostrich farm, anyone?) and you wanted to get your hands on your money, that's just too bad. You'll only be able to do so if you can demonstrate severe financial hardship.

$ *Super laws are confusing.* Have a read through any of the Australian Taxation Office's (ATO) lengthy publications on super and we guarantee you'll be asleep in no time (excellent for insomniacs!). All you really need to think about is getting the basics right and leave super laws to the experts.

$ *The rules could change.* As we all know, governments are notorious for changing their minds. Who knows what the rules governing super will be in 20, 30 or 40 years' time? It's impossible to tell. That said, it's unlikely that future governments will remove the great incentives for people to save for their own retirement as it takes the pressure off the public purse—and that's good for everyone.

The poor old pension

While a strong social security system is an important safety net for the disadvantaged, it's alarming to note that 2.3 million Australians over the age of 65 (or 77 per cent of people in this age group) currently receive some kind of income support from the government, including the age pension.

In 2010 the pension brings in a maximum fortnightly payment of around $670 for singles (about $17 400 per year) and around $1010 for couples (about $26 250 per year), both well below the levels required for a fun retirement. Unfortunately, the number of people turning to the pension is only likely to increase as our population ages and as retirees discover that they need assistance to prop up their meagre savings. In a nutshell, it's fair to say that the pension:

$ is not enough to sustain a comfortable retirement

$ might one day only be available to people who can demonstrate extreme hardship

$ should not be relied upon as a means of funding your retirement.

Sorting out your super: how much money do you have, and where is it?

Hopefully by now we've inspired (or scared) you into doing something about your super. Start by dusting off your piles of paperwork, and gathering together all the forms you've collected from your super funds over the years. You'll need these to work out exactly where all your super is, how much you have invested, the type of fund or funds you're in, how they're performing and how much you're paying in fees.

There are more super funds out there than IT professionals on rsvp.com, but most use a managed fund as the underlying investment (where your money is pooled with other people's money and invested by a professional fund manager—to understand how managed funds work make sure you check out chapter 6).

Types of investment options within super funds

Most super funds offer a number of different investment options to choose from—single-sector funds (those that invest in one asset class such as only cash or only shares, for example) or multi-sector funds (those that invest in a mixture of asset classes, such as cash, property and shares). It's important to make sure you're in the right type of fund based on your age and circumstances, because the varying returns made by different funds could have a huge impact on the size of your super balance come retirement time. There are three main types of multi-sector super funds:

$ *Conservative or defensive funds* usually hold most of their money in low-risk assets such as fixed interest with a small percentage in higher-risk growth assets such as property or shares. They generally pay steady but low returns.

$ *Balanced funds* usually hold around half of their money in low-risk assets (such as cash) and half in higher-risk growth assets such as property and shares.

$ *Growth funds* usually hold most of their money in Australian and international shares with a smaller percentage in property and cash. Over the long term, growth funds generally pay higher returns than conservative and balanced funds.

Workers with a decade or more until retirement should think about going for growth, as these funds have historically paid the highest returns over the long term and, as you have time on your side, you can ride out any sharemarket fluctuation.

Watch the default

It's important to note that your super fund trustee will probably have put your funds into a balanced fund by default if you didn't specify which option you wanted when you originally signed up. If that doesn't suit, you should fix this up quick smart and ask your fund manager to change it. Most super funds allow you to change the type of fund your money is invested in online — it's really just as simple as logging in and reviewing what type of fund you're currently in, and then changing it in a few swift clicks.

Other terms that you should be aware of

When investing in superannuation, it helps if you understand some of the jargon associated with the different types of funds. Here are some of the more common terms you'll come across on your superannuation adventures.

Industry versus retail super funds

You've probably been unable to escape those industry super fund ads on free-to-air TV — you know, the ones that make you want to call up immediately and get Foxtel? Originally set up by employer associations and trade unions, industry super funds started pushing the benefits of their funds around 2005 when a change in government legislation meant that for the first time employees could choose where their employer paid their super. The fear was that workers would leave in droves and join fancier retail super funds in the hope of achieving higher returns. The main benefit of industry funds is that they charge lower fees than your average retail fund because they don't pay commissions to financial advisers. While some industry funds are only open to workers in certain industries, most of the big funds will happily accept members regardless of their profession. They often perform very strongly, so they're definitely worth checking out.

Alternatively, you can join a retail super fund. They are offered by most of the big financial institutions in Australia, and anyone can join. There seem to be about a million different funds on offer so you're bound to find one that suits you. Many of them perform very well, but some retail super funds charge like wounded bulls — so make sure you take this into account when you're choosing a fund. For more information on investing in managed funds check out chapter 6.

Some of the big industry super fund managers in Australia are:

$ AustralianSuper: <www.australiansuper.com>

$ CareSuper: <www.caresuper.com.au>

$ Hesta Super Fund: <www.hesta.com.au>

$ Media Super: <www.mediasuper.com.au>.

Some of the popular retail super fund managers in Australia are:

$ Australian Ethical Investment: <www.australianethical.com.au>

$ Colonial First State: <www.colonialfirststate.com.au>

$ MLC: <www.mlc.com.au>

$ Perpetual: <www.perpetual.com.au>.

Self managed super funds

As the name implies, these funds let you control your own super by investing in a wide range of investments including shares and property. You'll need professional financial advice to set one up and operate it within the law — and that can be expensive. The Australian Securities and Investments Commission (ASIC) recommends that you have a minimum of around $200 000 invested in super to make this worthwhile. If you think self managed super might be up your alley, speak to your accountant — we tell you where you can find one in the 'Help when you need it' section at the back of this book.

Does your fund have a good track record?

Check to see if your fund has a history of performing well over the medium to long term and compare it to similar funds offered by other super fund managers. If you're in an investment option in your fund that invests only in Australian shares, you should compare it with the investment options in other super funds that invest solely in Australian shares.

Psst ...

Comparing super funds

An easy way to compare super funds is to check the one-, three- and five-year returns (where available) that are listed at the back of each month's *Smart Investor* magazine (published by the *Australian Financial Review*), in the financial pages of the big newspapers or online at <www.morningstar.com.au>. Morningstar also provides independent ratings of super funds, awarding star ratings out of five.

How much are you paying in fees?

Most super funds charge a combination of entry fees, annual management fees and exit fees. However the type of fees and the amount charged can vary widely between funds. Traditionally, retail super funds charge more than industry super funds partly because they usually pay commissions to financial advisers, something that industry super funds don't do. However most industry super funds also charge a small weekly fee (around one to two dollars per week) regardless of the account balance, and this can add up over time — it's particularly bad for those people whose super is spread over a number of funds.

The impact of fees on your final super balance can be startling, so it's very important that you understand exactly how much you're paying your fund manager. Even a difference of 1 per cent in annual management fees can make a massive difference in the long run.

Comparing the effect of fees over time

Let's say you earn an average salary of $40 000, and your employer contributes 9 per cent into your super without missing a beat for the next 40 years. If everything else is equal, take a look at what a 1 per cent difference in annual fees might make (shown in figure 7.1).

Figure 7.1: the effect of fees on superannuation performance

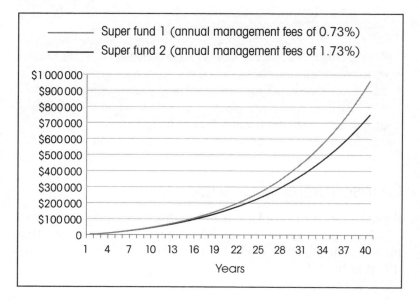

Super fund 1:
Annual fees: 0.73 per cent
Annual growth: 8 per cent
Value of investment after 40 years: $961452

Super fund 2:
Annual fees: 1.73 per cent
Annual growth: 8 per cent
Value of investment after 40 years: $750524

Difference: $210928

Of course, this is a simplified example and doesn't take into account things such as tax, salary hikes (or dips!) or if you take time out of the workplace, but it is certainly food for thought. If the fees are high, it's important that your fund consistently performs well; otherwise you might be better off somewhere else. Think of it like you would any other service you pay for: you want to get value for your money.

FIDO's risk and return calculator

If you want to calculate an accurate superannuation figure for your own circumstances, check out ASIC's consumer website FIDO's calculator: <www.fido.gov.au>. Just key in your investment choice and how many years you expect to be investing and it'll give you an idea as to how much you'll have at the end.

Consolidate your super

If you're like most people, you'll probably have worked a number of jobs over the years without keeping track of your super. That means your super is likely to be spread over one, two or 10 different funds!

If you have more than one super fund, it's a good idea to get it all under control by rolling everything over into one fund. This will make it easy to keep an eye on your balance and to see how you're tracking against target.

The question is: which fund should you choose? Start by working out where your money is at the moment. That's right, put your rubber gloves on and dig your paperwork out from the bottom of the budgie cage. Then do a bit of investigation. For example, has one of your funds performed consistently well over a number of years? Have a look at your fund statements and check out the Morningstar data at the back of *Smart Investor* magazine for help with this.

Whichever fund you choose, make sure it suits your goals and profile. For example, if you're young, you should seriously consider a growth fund (that is, one that's likely to generate the highest returns for you in the long term). If none of your funds are currently invested in growth, you should consider switching your money over to the growth option offered by one of your current fund managers (choose a fund that's performed well over as long a time frame as possible) and roll all of your super into this fund.

Once you've decided which fund (or funds) you'd like to stick with, it's just a matter of rolling your other super funds over. It's pretty simple really: just jump onto your preferred fund's website and download a super rollover form. This gives them the authorisation to request a transfer of your super from any of your old funds.

Chase that super

There are millions of dollars floating around the bowels of Australian financial institutions in the form of unclaimed superannuation. Luckily, there's an easy way to find out if any of it is yours. The SuperSeeker section on the ATO website <www.ato.gov.au> lets you run a quick online check—you'll need to provide your name, date of birth and tax file number. If you do dig anything up, simply roll this money into your preferred super fund.

Boosting your super: ways to go about it

Depending on your age and circumstances, contributing extra to your super might be a good or not-so-good idea. Here's a rough guide:

$ *If you're in your 20s*, there are bound to be a million other things you'd rather be doing with your money — exploring the world perhaps, or saving for a house deposit. But if you're über-organised and want to get a head start (making the most of our good friend, compound interest), go for it. Small, regular, voluntary contributions would be the way to go.

$ *If you've hit your 30s*, you're probably busy paying off a mortgage, but now is a good time to start making regular, voluntary contributions to your super if at all possible (and if you haven't already).

$ *If you're over 40* and you haven't already started making contributions — giddy-up! Remember, the later you leave it the harder it's going to be to get your super into shape — you'll have to make much larger contributions than if you'd started earlier.

If you've decided to contribute to your super, there are several ways you can go about it, and we'll walk you through them now.

Salary sacrifice

While the word 'sacrifice' has rather negative connotations, salary sacrificing is a nifty way to boost your super. How does it work? Basically, you arrange for your employer to pay some of your pre-tax income into your super. (Have a chat to your HR manager at work about how this may impact your salary.) Some of the benefits are:

$ You'll reduce your taxable income, so you pay less tax.

$ It's forced saving — you don't spend what you never see.

Government co-contributions

If you earn less than $58 000 and you make a personal contribution to your super, you could be eligible to receive a co-contribution from the Australian Government of up to $1000. That's free money! Simply contact your super fund, make a voluntary personal contribution of up to $1000 (that's in after-tax dollars) and you should be eligible. The government will then make a contribution to your super depending on the amount you've invested yourself and how much you earn. You'll receive the money sometime after you've submitted your tax return for the financial year just passed — it'll be paid straight into your current super fund.

Psst ...

Keep an ear to the ground

Be warned: the government often changes the rules that govern things like the government co-contribution scheme and contribution tax thresholds, so be sure to keep an ear to the ground if super is your weapon of choice.

Spousal contributions

If you're not earning an income (perhaps you're a stay-at-home mum) or if you're a low-income earner, your partner can make a contribution into your super for you and this can be a great way to keep your super balance chugging along. If your partner makes a spousal contribution for you the good news is that you'll receive the government co-contribution as well. Hurrah!

Self-employed contributions

If you're self-employed and you're under 50, you can claim a tax deduction for any contributions you make to your super up to the limit of $50 000 per year.

Maree's story (age 48)

At the age of 48, superannuation is a very important part of my investment strategy.

Superannuation wasn't something I'd really thought about investing in back at the age of 21 when I started working for the government, but it just so happened that employer superannuation contributions were compulsory where I worked (unlike many other organisations that weren't required to make any payments until 1992). It's really paid off, because as a result of investing in my super when I was young, my balance has grown nicely.

Six years ago I really started to build my superannuation up after attending a talk about the financial benefits of salary sacrificing. Following this I joined an industry super fund and started making salary sacrificed contributions from my fortnightly pay. I now increase my super contributions whenever I get a pay rise as I know I'm not going to miss the money because I'm not used to receiving it.

One of the best things about salary sacrificing into super is the tax benefits, which are hard to beat. In addition to superannuation, I have investments in shares that I intend to increase over time—my aim is to derive a regular income from my shares (in the form of dividends) to boost my retirement income. I also plan to pay off my home mortgage prior to retiring.

I'm fortunate because unlike many other women, I know that I'll be able to fully support myself in a lifestyle of my choosing when I retire, because I've actively worked to increase my superannuation over the years—even if it wasn't a conscious choice while I was young.

My advice to other women is to start up a super fund when they get their first job and contribute whatever they can afford in order to receive the government co-contribution (if the government continues to offer it). The early contributions will grow over time and really boost their retirement savings. Even if you're working part time, it would be advantageous to use the co-contribution as it has a better return than saving via other means. I'd also recommend that women take the time to read about their superannuation fund and all the options it gives them. Super really is such an important investment.

Tax talk

While there's no limit to the amount of money you can amass in super, there are rules as to how much you can contribute every year before you're subject to extra tax.

If you're under the age of 50 you can make up to $25 000 worth of pre-tax contributions each year (this includes employer contributions) before you'll have to worry about paying extra tax. If you're under the age of 65, you can make up to $150 000 worth of post-tax contributions before being subject to extra tax (unlikely to be a problem for most of us!).

A couple can contribute up to $300 000 of post-tax contributions to their super before being subject to extra tax. The partner making the contribution could get a tax rebate on their income tax bill for any super contributions they make for their spouse — there are some conditions attached, so check this out with your accountant first.

Checklist: get on track for a fabulous future

Spring-cleaning your super will feel pretty good (we promise!) and pave the way for a happy retirement. If you've decided to take action, there are a few easy steps you can take that will help you to make the most of your super:

1   *Decide how much money you'd like to retire on.* Decide on your ideal annual salary as if you were to retire tomorrow. If you're young, aim high and give yourself something to work towards. If you're not sure what's realistic, remember that industry bodies suggest an annual income of $39 000 (after tax) for a single or $52 000 for a couple will support a comfy retirement in 2010. Remember that if you're young and light-years away from retirement you'll have to review the figure you're aiming for, and make sure that you regularly increase it to account for inflation.

Work out how much you'll have to contribute to your super to reach your target by using a superannuation calculator — try the calculator at <www.fido.gov.au>.

2   *Find out if you're in the right kind of fund to help you reach your goals.* Where is your super now, and how much do you have? Are you in the right kind of fund for your age and personal circumstances? Are you in the right investment option in your super fund — a more conservative option (if you're close to retirement age) or aggressive (if you're a long way from retirement and want your money to grow like string beans)? If you haven't specified your investment option your super fund trustee has probably stuck your money in a balanced investment option by default. This might not be appropriate for your unique scenario, so check out your paperwork and contact your super fund if you want to make a change.

Also consider how much you are paying in fees and how your fund is performing. These factors could have an enormous impact on your final super balance years down the track. If you're not sure on either count, check on your fund's website. Have a look at Morningstar's ratings and returns at the back of *Smart Investor* magazine, in the financial pages of the big newspapers or on Morningstar's website <www.morningstar.com.au>.

3   *Spring clean your super.* Once you've decided on the super fund for you, roll over any other super you have into that fund. It's very easy: just log on to your preferred fund's website, download a rollover form, fill it out and send it off. They'll then take care of it for you. Also make sure that your super fund has your tax file number on file. That way you won't be slugged with any unnecessary tax.

Check to see if there's any lost super in your name — enter your details in the SuperSeeker section of the ATO website <www.ato.gov.au> and bingo!

4   *Top up your super and watch it grow.* If it's dawned on you
      that it's going to take a bit of work to get your super
      balance up to scratch and you'd like to make extra
      contributions, there's no time like the present. Think
      about salary sacrificing (organise this with the help of your
      HR manager at work) or make an after-tax contribution
      and get the government co-contribution every year.

      If you have a partner and are either not going out to
      work yourself or are a low-income earner, talk to him or
      her about making contributions to your super. If you're
      self-employed it's important that you make your own
      contributions to your super whenever possible.

5   *Track that super!* Be a girl scout and keep all of your bits
      and bobs — that is, statements and paperwork — in the
      one place. If you have the stomach for it, regularly check
      that all of your super payments are hitting your super
      fund. It should say on each of your pay slips how much
      super your employer has contributed for that pay period
      and you should cross-check this with the statements
      you receive from your super fund (or check the member
      section of your fund's website). Mistakes have been known
      to happen. Keep in mind that there's likely to be a time
      delay with employer contributions and they may hit your
      account in a lump sum every two or three months rather
      than just after every pay.

Remember: always ask for help if you need it

If you feel you need help sorting out your super, you should see
a licensed financial adviser sooner rather than later. We tell you
where you can find one in the 'Help when you need it' section at
the back of this book.

chapter 8

property

There once was a girl called Simone
Who wanted to buy her first home
She saved for two years
(no coffee or beers!)
And now she's approved for a loan.

It would be easy for an outsider to get the impression that Australians are obsessed with real estate: we talk about it, buy magazines and books about it, watch television shows about it and spend a lot of time planning how to get our hands on it. According to the Australian Bureau of Statistics, around 70 per cent of households currently either own their own home or are in the process of paying it off — that's one of the highest rates of home ownership in the world. In this chapter we'll cover:

$ property 101: buying residential property

$ buying a home: a place to live in and call your own

$ buying investment property: becoming a property mogul

$ checklist: buying that property.

At a glance

Here's a snapshot of six things you might like to know about buying property.

→ **Who is best suited to buying property?** Property is tangible, so it appeals to people who like to be able to 'see' where their money has gone. It's especially good for those of us lucky enough to have been born with the home renovator gene.

→ **How much money do I need to start?** Generally you'll need 20 per cent of the purchase price to buy your first property, plus enough to cover stamp duty (a state or territory government tax) and other costs. As a rough guide, if you're planning on buying a property in New South Wales worth $440 000, you'll need to come up with $88 000 for the deposit and around $15 500 in stamp duty — plus up to $1000 in bank fees and around $1000 for a solicitor.

→ **How much money can I expect to make?** Property prices in most areas of Australia have historically risen steadily over the long term (in 1999 the average house price in capital cities was $167 000 — by 2009 it had jumped to $440 000) although in the short term you could hear about prices in one area booming while others have flat lined or even fallen in value. If you're lucky enough to buy a property in an area that takes off, you could make a tidy packet if you decide to sell.

→ **What kind of time frame works best when buying property?** Ranges from short term (under a year if you buy to renovate then sell quickly) to long term (years or decades) if you're buying a family home or an investment property from which you'd like to receive an income down the track.

→ **How much work goes into buying property?** The workload is high. Making a smart property purchase takes time and effort plus you'll have to cope with a mountain of paperwork. Once it's yours, you'll also have to make sure it's well maintained.

→ **Look out for:** dodgy real estate agents. While there are many good, honest agents around, there must be enough of the unsavoury variety to have given that profession such a bad reputation. Just keep your wits about you and always do your own research.

Property 101: buying residential property

Property makes a pretty attractive investment option: it's tangible (so you can tinker with it to your heart's content); it's a relatively stable kind of investment (compared with shares, for example); it can give you tax advantages; and, if you have enough equity built up in a property, banks will usually let you borrow money against it. Most of us also know a little bit about property, which makes it an easy type of investment to understand.

Huh?

Equity

When we're talking about property, the term 'equity' refers to the value of the property you own, after the cost of anything owed against it has been deducted. So if a house you own is worth $350 000 and you owe $250 000, you have $100 000 equity.

You can buy a home to live in, an investment property to rent out or you can buy a commercial property — that is, office buildings and the like (although we'll be focusing on residential property in this chapter).

Property has historically performed very strongly in Australia, particularly in capital cities. If you need convincing, take a look at figure 8.1 (overleaf), which shows median house prices in Australia over the past 30 years.

Figure 8.1: median house prices in Australia since 1981

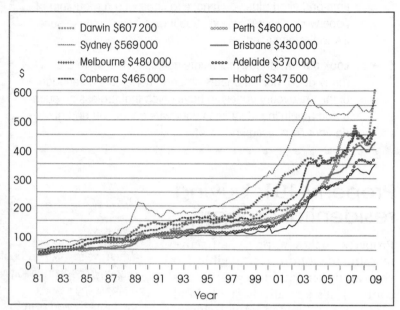

Is the great Australian dream over?

There's no escaping the fact that rising property prices are making it harder and harder for the average person to afford their own home. At some point in the future it's possible that property ownership, at least in our major cities, will be well and truly out of most people's reach.

So just how much has the situation changed over the past three decades?

$ *Then*: in 1979 the average house price in Australian capital cities was around $39000.

$ *Now*: at the end of 2009, it had risen to around $440000.

Back in the 1970s the average house price in Australian capital cities was around three to four times the average worker's earnings — by 2007 it had risen to over seven times average earnings. In other words, property is now a lot more expensive relative to our incomes, it's taking more money to service the average home loan and longer to pay it off.

It's not all doom and gloom

If you don't yet own a property but want to get your hands on one, it's certainly not all bad news. The Australian population is growing, fuelling a need for more housing — and that's good news for property owners.

You mightn't be able to afford a house on a quarter acre block in a nice suburb like your parents did when they were starting out. But with demand for housing increasing and the shift to higher-density housing likely to continue, there are still plenty of opportunities to get into the property market, not only in capital cities but also in regional areas. It might just be a case of lowering your expectations and starting small. After all, you don't want your quality of life to suffer because you're spending every available cent paying off a huge mortgage. If you're going to take the plunge, be sensible!

Buying versus renting — the great debate

The relative pros and cons of buying as opposed to renting are contentious and you'll find financial experts who'll argue either side of the coin.

On the one hand, there are those who argue that mortgages force people to save money they probably would otherwise have spent. On the other, some suggest that home owners are spending too much paying off huge interest bills and that over time they'd be better off renting and investing the difference between their rent and what they would have paid on their mortgage — perhaps in shares, for example.

If you're the kind of person who could benefit from a dose of forced saving, a mortgage could be just the ticket; but if you're a bit of a squirrel and have no problem budgeting and saving, you might be better off investing your money elsewhere.

The million-dollar question

If you've decided that property is your cup of tea, you need to ask yourself why you want to buy it. That might sound strange, but it's important; the answer will have a significant impact on the type of property you buy and where you buy it. Only you can decide what suits you best, so take some time to answer the following questions:

$ Do you want to buy a home to live in or an investment property to rent out?

$ Do you want to buy a brand-spanking new property or are you interested in buying something old and living the *Better Homes and Gardens* renovating dream?

$ Do you want to buy a property locally or are you after something in another state or territory?

When you've answered these questions, you'll be well placed to begin your hunt for a property.

Jump online

If you're not sure what type of property you'd like to buy, start to suss out what's on the market. It might help clear things up for you. You'll quickly work out what's out there and at around what price. An easy way to start your search is to go online: this is one of the fun bits when it comes to buying property. Perhaps even more fun are the house inspections—while time-consuming they can become addictive!

Property online

There are a number of websites dedicated to helping you search for property and these are some of the biggies. Some of them will let you register for email alerts so you'll receive an email whenever anything new matching your specifications comes onto the market. Don't be surprised to see the same property pop up on different websites. Here are some of our favourites:

→ Buy My Place: <www.buymyplace.com.au>

→ Domain: <www.domain.com.au>

→ Homehound: <www.homehound.com.au>

→ Property.com.au: <www.property.com.au>

→ Realestate.com.au: <www.realestate.com.au>.

The good, the bad and the ugly

Like all the other types of investment, there are some pluses and minuses when it comes to buying property, and here they are.

The good:

$ *A mortgage = forced saving.* If you're paying off a mortgage, especially if you're working hard at it to pay your loan off quickly, you're effectively forcing yourself to invest your hard-earned money. That's money you might have spent if you'd been renting.

$ *Property is tangible.* You can see it and touch it and you have something to show for your money. If you're a property owner you can get your kicks showing your place off to your friends and you can join in on discussions about renovating at dinner parties. Priceless.

$ *Tax breaks and happy bankers.* Owning property can give you tax breaks. Plus, depending on how much equity you have built up in a property (as well as other factors such as how much you earn and how much other debt you have), banks will usually let you borrow money against it.

The bad (and the ugly):

§ *The expense.* Property isn't cheap, and it usually requires a substantial outlay. Plus you'll be up for costs including stamp duty and legal fees, all of which add up (don't forget you'll have to maintain your property, too). If you took out a hefty mortgage you could also be paying a lot more in interest than you would've been paying in rent — that's money you could have invested elsewhere.

§ *Poor liquidity.* If and when you come to sell your property, it's likely to take some time before you get your hands on your money. Even if you've got a buyer lined up, it could still take months for the property to be settled.

§ *Lack of diversification.* If you've used a good chunk of your savings towards a house deposit (which is likely if you're a first home buyer) and then continue to spend most of your cash on mortgage repayments, it means you're putting all of your eggs in one basket rather than spreading your money around different investments. That could be an issue down the track.

Buying a home: a place to live in and call your own

Unfortunately, buying a home in real life isn't as simple as playing Monopoly. If you land on Park Lane you'll have to do more than just check it's not owned before you buy it from the bank — it's going to take time and effort!

Location, location, location?

Despite the old adage you'll often hear bandied about by real estate agents, location isn't everything: there are other things to consider, too. When you're buying a house that you plan to make your home, your personal preferences are going to come into play. However, remember that while you mightn't mind living under that flight path, plenty of other people will — and that could make your home harder to sell in the future. Property that's close to public transport, schools and shops is always likely to be in demand, while you might find it harder to sell a property if it comes with a swimming pool or tennis court (basically, any feature that requires constant maintenance). Just use your common sense.

Financing your dream home

There are a number of things to consider when financing your dream home and we'll walk you through them now.

How much will you need?

How much are you going to have to save to put a deposit on that cute little cottage with the white picket fence? Generally, lenders require you to come up with 20 per cent of the purchase price yourself plus enough to cover purchase costs. So if you want to buy a $440 000 property, you'll need $88 000 as a deposit, as well as costs (the main ones being stamp duty, bank fees and solicitor's fees). Be warned: stamp duty can be very nasty (stamp duty rates are covered overleaf). Bank fees will vary between lenders (budget for $500 to $1000) and solicitors will usually charge around $1000 — make sure you ask for a written quote before they start any work for you.

As property prices are rising higher and higher, it's getting harder to save 20 per cent of the purchase price — or rather, it's taking longer to get there. Although it is advisable to save 20 per cent (to try to take out as small a mortgage as possible) some lenders will let you borrow 90 per cent and in some cases even 100 per cent of the purchase price (not a great idea if you don't fancy spending most of your working life paying it off!). If you do decide to borrow more than 80 per cent of the purchase price, be warned: you'll then be required to pay lender's mortgage insurance, which protects the lender (not you) in case you default on your loan payments. Your lender will tell you exactly how much it's going to cost you, but it generally comes in at around 1 per cent of the total loan. So if you're buying a property worth $440 000 and you're borrowing 90 per cent of the purchase cost ($396 000), you'll be hit with an extra $3960 in costs — and that's just in the first year.

On the day you actually buy the property and sign the contract — whether that be just after the auction or after you've negotiated an agreed price with the seller — you usually have to put up 10 per cent of the purchase price as a deposit immediately. Speak to your lender about organising finance for this beforehand if you're not using your own cash or if you'll require a cheque on the day.

Stamp duty

Stamp duty is a tax you'll have to pay whenever you buy a property. The amount you pay will depend on the cost of the property and where you buy (rates are set by the state or territory governments) but to give you an idea, the stamp duty payable on a $440 000 property (including mortgage registration fee and transfer fee) in January 2010 was:

→ ACT: $17 485 → QLD: $7582 → VIC: $19 670
→ NSW: $15 575 → SA: $21 191 → WA: $15 225
→ NT: $19 532 → TAS: $15 367

To make your own calculations, you'll find a stamp duty calculator on the websites of most of the big lenders.

Get friendly with your mortgage

You'll need to do a bit of work when it comes to finding the right mortgage for you. There seem to be a mind-boggling number of options on the market, but don't panic: they're fairly basic, just with different bells and whistles. There are several types of mortgage available — here's a bit about each:

§ *Fixed interest rate loans* will lock in the interest rate for a set period (usually anywhere from six months to 10 years), which is a good option if you're the type who won't be able to sleep at night if there's talk that interest rates might go up. They can, however, be quite inflexible, for example by restricting the amount of extra repayments you can make each year.

§ *Variable interest rate loans* rise or fall with interest rate movements. The rates charged are completely at the discretion of lenders, but they typically reflect changes to the official interest rate set by the Reserve Bank of Australia. Variable rates are generally a little lower than the shortest-term fixed rate offered by a lender.

§ *Split home loans* allow you to take part of your loan as a fixed interest and part as a variable interest, which is good for people who like the peace of mind that comes with fixed but the flexibility of a variable. Your lender or mortgage broker will be able to help you decide what suits you best.

Interest rates

Interest rates are a moveable feast and it's impossible to accurately predict when they'll rise or fall, or by how much. While in 2009 the variable interest rate hit a low of 5.55 per cent, back in 1990 it hovered around an all-time high of 17 per cent—ouch! Hopefully a high interest rate like that will never darken our doorsteps again, but who knows?

When you take out a mortgage the amount you borrow is referred to as the principal. Whether you pay off the principal and the interest as part of your repayment scheme, or just the interest, is a decision you'll have to make when selecting a loan.

There are pros and cons to both types of loans:

$ *Principal and interest loans* require you to pay interest every month, as well as a portion of the principal, so gradually you pay off your loan until you owe nothing. In our opinion, this is a smart way to go when buying your own home.

$ *Interest-only loans* are becoming common, but are best left to people who are investing in property rather than buying a home to live in themselves. With this type of loan, the mortgage never gets any smaller as it's only the interest that's paid every month — the principal is never reduced. The reasoning behind taking out a loan like this is that, when you eventually sell the property, the profit you make will more than cover the interest you've paid.

$ *Mortgage offset accounts* link your mortgage to a special everyday transaction account called an 'offset account' and any money sitting in this account is then offset against your loan. So let's say you have a mortgage of $280 000 with $20 000 sitting in your offset account. The lender will only charge you interest on $260 000. The amount of interest you pay will increase and decrease as the amount in your offset account falls or rises in value. Offset accounts are used exactly like everyday transaction accounts for every other purpose. For example, most people would have their wage paid into this account. The more money you have in your offset account, the less interest you pay. Nice! Mortgage offset accounts also give you tax advantages, as you won't be paying tax on any interest that your $20 000 would have earned over the year if it had been in a savings account or a term deposit.

Which mortgage is for you?

There are some great websites that can help you compare mortgages and point out any great offers on the market. Try <www.moneymanager.com.au> or <www.ratecity.com.au>.

A helping hand

If you plan on buying a home to live in and you've never owned property in your name before you could be eligible for the government's First Home Owner Grant (conditions apply) and you could also be eligible for concessions on stamp duty. Your lender will have all the forms you need to fill out to apply for this.

The First Home Owner Grant's lesser-known little sister is the First Home Saver Account. In short, the government will make capped contributions to a special home savings account that you set up based on how much you contribute yourself. There are other benefits too, like paying less tax on your earnings. For details of the scheme and to see if you're eligible check out ASIC's consumer website, FIDO: <www.fido.gov.au>.

Before you sign

There are a few important things you'll need to take care of before you commit to a mortgage on a property. We'll discuss some of the big ones over the next few pages.

Research

Once you've got your finance sorted and you're out in the market (finally!), you should research as widely as possible to make sure you have a realistic idea as to how much you're going to have to pay to buy a house, unit or apartment in any particular area. Comprehensive research will require you to attend auctions, check out the auction results in Sunday's newspapers, have a look at property websites and ask people you know who might have already bought in that area. Do not rely solely on advice from real estate agents!

Building and pest inspections

When you think you might have found your dream home, consider getting a building and pest inspection carried out. This will give you peace of mind, and could save you serious cash down the track if that 'renovator's delight' (real estate agent speak for 'a dump') turns out to be a little less delightful than you'd imagined. The cost of these inspections will vary depending on the location and type of property, but for around $600 you'll receive a written report that rates the current condition of a property, details any problems and estimates how much it's likely to cost to get them fixed. Try Archicentre: <www.archicentre.com.au>.

Negotiating with a seller versus buying at auction

You'll need to consider doing things a little differently if you're buying your property at auction rather than negotiating with a seller. If you're buying a property at auction, for example, you won't want to be forking out to have a property inspected if there's a good chance you're not going to end up the buyer. If you're *very* confident that come auction day you're going to be cracking open the champagne, think about getting a building and pest inspection done before the auction. Try to organise it on the sly to avoid letting the real estate agent know how keen you are — ask the inspector to arrange it directly with the agent and send them in on their own. You should already have a realistic idea as to what kind of price a property will go for at auction based on your research, so in this case an independent valuation might not be necessary.

Independent valuation

There are professionals who specialise in property valuations, and who aren't trying to sell you anything. It's always a good idea to get an unbiased opinion as to what a property is really worth — that way you can be assured you're not going to be paying too much. The cost of an independent valuation will vary depending on the location and type of property, however you should be able to get one done for around \$400. Try Herron Todd White: <www.htw.com.au>.

Psst ...

Contract of sale clauses

A contract of sale is a written agreement that sets out all of the conditions surrounding a property sale (signed by both seller and buyer). If you're negotiating with a seller to buy a property, seriously consider adding two clauses to specify that your offer is subject to a satisfactory building and pest inspection and a satisfactory independent valuation.

After you sign

Don't think that the hard work is over when you sign on the dotted line! There are still a few things you'll need to organise to ensure things go as smoothly as possible during the transition phase after you've bought the property to the day you pick up the keys. Here are some of the big ones.

Huh?

Conveyancing

Conveyancing is a fancy-pants term for the paper pushing of all of the legal documents involved when a property is sold. Your solicitor will check all of the documents affecting the transfer of your property (the property title and the like) from the seller to the buyer (you!) and make sure everything is above board.

Huh?

Body corporate

In apartment buildings and blocks of units, all the owners of the individual apartments in the building get together and elect a group of people to maintain the building or block of units. This group is called a 'body corporate'. Owners pay regular fees to the body corporate to cover the building's expenses, from building insurance to gardening and repair of common areas of the building.

Employ a solicitor

You'll need a solicitor to carry out your conveyancing work. If you don't already have a solicitor, we tell you where you can find one in the 'Help when you need it' section at the back of this book.

Take out insurance — immediately

It's very important that your property is covered by insurance from the day on which you officially buy it, because you'll now have an interest in it. You should make sure that the building, fittings and fixtures are covered. If you're buying a property that has a body corporate, the building will already be covered by the body corporate's insurance — but you'll still need to make sure you have insurance that covers any fittings and fixtures in your own apartment or unit. Once you move in you should also make sure your contents are covered.

Now get to work paying your mortgage off!

The interest rate and the number of years it takes to pay off your mortgage will have a huge impact on the total cost of the loan. Any extra repayments you are able to make mean a shorter loan term, and could save you *a lot* of money. Paying the mortgage off in the shortest possible period of time should be the goal of anyone taking out a loan to buy their own home. Consider the scenario depicted below to get a rough idea of how much you could save by paying your mortgage off quickly.

Example: paying off a mortgage in 15 years rather than 25 years

Let's say you buy a house for $440 000. After putting down an $88 000 deposit and paying your stamp duty and costs, you take out a loan for $352 000 with an average annual interest rate of 7.5 per cent. Take a look at figure 8.2 to see the difference paying off your loan in 15 years versus 25 years could make.

Figure 8.2: interest paid on 15-year loan versus 25-year loan

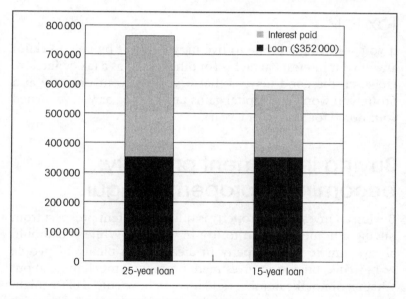

25-year loan: Monthly repayments: $2601
        Total paid: $780 375 (of which $428 375 is interest)

15-year loan: Monthly repayments: $3263
        Total paid: $587 355 (of which $235 355 is interest)

As you can see, if you paid the loan back in 15 years rather than 25, you could save up to $193 000.

Online mortgage repayment calculators

If you want to see the difference that paying off your loan over different time frames makes, jump online and use a mortgage repayment calculator. The federal government's consumer finance website has a good one: <www.understandingmoney.gov.au>. Be sure to check out the difference fortnightly repayments might make, too.

Tax talk

If you're buying a home to live in, you won't be able to claim any of your interest payments (or other costs) as a tax deduction. However, the good news is that if you sell your property at a profit, you won't pay capital gains tax (as long as you've owned your home for at least one year).

Buying investment property: becoming a property mogul

Buying an investment property is quite a different prospect from buying a home you plan to live in yourself. While you should always aim to buy property in areas where plenty of people want to live, buying an investment property is much more about whether or not the numbers add up than how 'cute' a place might be or how much it might appeal to your personal taste. The trick when buying investment property is to not get emotionally attached to any particular place. Remember, if you get beaten to the post and miss out on a property you had your eye on, don't stress, there'll be another just around the corner—plenty more fish in the sea.

Two key things you'll need to assess when buying investment property are:

$ *Income*: how much rent an investment property will bring in, including your likely tax return

$ *Capital growth*: the amount by which the property is likely to increase in value over time.

In order to help you successfully assess whether you can make the numbers work with any particular property you might have in mind, you'll have to educate yourself about property investment. Start by reading some of the great books specialising in property investment that are on the market — we've listed them at the end of this chapter. Also remember to check out property investment websites such as:

$ Destiny: <www.destiny.com.au>

$ Propertywomen.com: <www.propertywomen.com.au>

$ Wakelin Property Advisory: <www.wakelin.com.au>.

Note that the philosophies of some property investors are quite different to others, so it's a good idea to read widely in order to help you to decide what you might like to do.

Positive and negative gearing

As you start down the path to becoming a property mogul you'll regularly hear terms such as negative gearing, positive gearing and positive cash flow mentioned. These concepts are quite easy to understand, but can obviously be confusing if you've never heard them before! Here's a basic explanation of each:

$ *Negative gearing* occurs when the rent generated by a property does not cover the property's expenses (interest on the mortgage and all other costs). In other words, the property owner loses money on the investment. The only way of recouping these losses is to hope that the property increases in value over time so that when it's sold the profit (after tax) will cover all of these losses and hopefully more.

$ *Positive gearing* occurs when a property's rent more than covers the expenses. In this case, the property owner makes money and has to pay tax on their profit.

$ *Positive cash flow* occurs when the expenses on a negatively geared property provide a tax return that more than covers these expenses. Positive cash flow therefore generates a profit on the property, the income of which is not taxed because it's been generated from a tax return. For more information about this, read the property investment books of Margaret Lomas.

While the ultimate aim of a property investor should be to own positively geared, or property on which positive cash flow is received, it can be tricky to find such property — especially if interest rates are high and mortgages cost a lot to service. You really have to know what you're doing and what to look for — and that's where your research comes in.

Research as widely as you can

Research is the key to making a good investment property purchase. To help you get started, we've listed some of the main avenues open to you when it comes to getting to know the property market:

$ *Surf the web*. The great thing about the internet is that you can easily search for property to buy anywhere in Australia without leaving your house. You can also check out properties for rent on the same websites, and that makes it pretty easy to see if there's a scarcity or glut of rental properties in any particular suburb or town.

$ *Talk to local property managers*. Property managers are real estate agents who focus on managing rental property rather than selling. Talk to property managers in the area in which you're looking and they should be able to let you know what the local conditions are like. For example, they'll help you answer important questions such as:

→   Is there much demand for rental property in the area?

→   What kind of property is in demand (for example, four bedroom houses or two bedroom apartments)?

→   What kind of rent can you expect to make?

$ *Talk to other investors.* It's always a good idea to talk to other people who've invested in the area and even talk to the locals, too if you can — just to find out what's going on.

Location, location, location

When you're buying an investment property rather than a home to live in, you don't have the added pressure of having to 'love' the property you buy; it's all about working out how much income the property will generate in comparison to expenses, and trying to predict whether it will appreciate in value over the time you own it (particularly if you're only planning on holding it for the short term). Consider buying investment property that's near public transport, schools and shops, near universities and hospitals (or in any area that has a high demand for rental properties) and in areas showing strong signs of growth. You can get tips from the monthly *Australian Property Investor* magazine and there are often articles in the daily newspapers, or talk to other property investors you might know.

Psst ...

Buy near Bunnings

Big chains such as Bunnings Warehouse spend a fortune on market research before deciding where to build new stores. They only build in areas that show excellent prospects for growth, and you can make the most of their hard work and plonk yourself down in the same suburb or town—make sure you do all your other research too, though! To get some ideas, have a look at their website to see where their new stores are located and where they'll be opening soon.

Don't forget that different types of investment property are going to be sought after in different locations. For example, in areas close to universities you might find that one-bedroom apartments are in high demand as rentals whereas in suburban areas three- or four-bedroom houses might be all the rage.

Financing your investment property

When it comes to organising finance for an investment property purchase you'll find that you have to cover the same costs that you would if you were buying a home to live in. However financing your property purchase will be slightly different (as will the tax implications of your investment). Read on for more information.

How much will you need?

When you're buying an investment property, you have to come up with 20 per cent of the purchase price (plus enough to cover purchase costs — roughly 5 per cent of the purchase price). If this is your first property, the money will have to come out of your own pocket. However if you already own or partly own your home (or another investment property), you can use the equity you've built up in the existing property instead of dipping into your savings.

Your lender will be able to tell you how much you're eligible to borrow. Keep in mind that you'll still have to demonstrate that you can service the loan based on how much money you have coming in (including income from other investment properties) as well as how much other debt you have to service.

In exactly the same way as if you were buying a home to live in, the other main upfront costs when you're buying an investment property are stamp duty, bank fees and solicitor's fees. You should also pay for a building and pest inspection and an independent valuation prior to signing any contract.

Note that as a property investor you're not eligible for the First Home Owner Grant or the First Home Saver Account.

Sharon's story (age 39)

As a child I was a keen saver, delighting in watching a growing balance in my school bank book. You could say my interest in investing started way back then! I became interested in property at the age of 30 when I befriended a man who had a passion for property investment (and who enthusiastically lent me his copy of Jan Somers' *Building Wealth through Investment Property*). This was a pivotal moment for me—a revelation. I witnessed him add to his growing portfolio of investment property and before long I was convinced of the wisdom of Jan's simple formula.

My first step was to talk to the banks about how much I could borrow and what repayments I could afford while still maintaining my current lifestyle. With my loan approved, I went looking for an 'entry level' property where my parents lived. It was a region that I could see was beginning to change and that I believe showed potential.

As a young, single property buyer I was underestimated by the local real estate agents, but I took on the challenge to secure the right property at the best price with enthusiasm (the agent still makes comment on the excellent price I got on my first property!). Six months later I felt as though I had the first property set up and managed, so I felt confident enough to buy my second property in the same area. Ten years later, both properties had approximately tripled in value and continue to provide a steady rental income.

Four years after my second property purchase and with a share portfolio under my belt, I was ready to buy a property I could live in. I purchased this property with my boyfriend. It was important to me that we approached the purchase as individuals so we found a loan that allowed us to split the ownership 50/50 whilst suiting our different financial positions. The two-bedroom art deco apartment we bought has proven to be an excellent investment.

In the last three years my now-husband and I have made two other property purchases, both of which we've lived in as our home. I think of all of our property purchases as investment decisions and I look forward to continuing my property investment story for a long time to come.

Get friendly with your mortgage

Interest only loans with mortgage offset accounts are great for people buying investment property. With this type of loan the principal never gets any smaller (as you're only paying the interest every month) so it means you'll keep more money in your pocket. That gives you greater cash flow and will make it easier to service another loan on another investment property (if you decide you'd like to buy one at some point). The extra cash will also make it easier to build up savings in your offset account that then reduces the amount of interest you pay on your loan every month.

The idea is that with time, the value of your property will increase — so if you sell it you'll be able to pay back the principal and make a profit. The rent will also increase over time to the point where it should be covering all of your costs and more. This will then provide you with an income if you decide to keep your property instead.

Before you sign

There are a few important things you'll need to take care of before you commit to buying an investment property. In particular, have a building and pest inspection and an independent valuation carried out to make sure you're not buying a lemon that's going to require a fortune in repairs in order to bring it up to scratch for tenants to live in, and to make sure you don't pay too much for any property. You should ask to have two clauses added to the contract of sale to specify that your offer is subject to a satisfactory building and pest inspection and a satisfactory independent valuation.

After you sign

In terms of paperwork, owning an investment property can be more work than owning your own home. Here are some of the things you'll need to swing into action to sort out once you've signed the contract.

Visit your friendly solicitor

You'll need to use the services of a solicitor for conveyancing when you're buying an investment property.

Take out insurance — immediately

In order to protect your interest in your new investment property, it's very important that your property is covered by insurance from the day on which you officially buy it. You should make sure that the building, fittings and fixtures are covered. If you're buying a property that has a body corporate, the building will already be covered by the body corporate's insurance but you'll still need to make sure you have insurance that covers any fittings and fixtures in your own apartment or unit. Once settlement has passed you should also take out landlord's insurance to cover you against theft, damage and liability by tenants as well as rent default and loss of rent.

Get a depreciation report

Once you've taken possession of the property, get a depreciation report done immediately — it'll cost you around $600 and that's tax deductible. Many of the fittings and fixtures (such as carpets, curtains and the stove in the kitchen) can be depreciated over a number of years — and this means more money in your pocket thanks to Australian taxation laws. If your residential property was built after 18 July 1985, you can also claim depreciation on the building itself. For more information about claiming depreciation on your next tax return, check out BMT & Assoc — Quantity Surveyors: <www.bmtqs.com.au>.

Hire a property manager

You've got a couple of options when it comes to having your investment property managed: you can do it yourself or you can pay a professional property manager to do it for you. This second option will take the stress off you, and you'll be able to claim any fees charged as a tax deduction — which makes it relatively inexpensive. Call several property managers in the area to compare their service and rates — they should be willing to negotiate on fees.

Visit your accountant

An accountant will be able to help you maximise allowable deductions on your investment property — don't forget to hand over your depreciation schedule to them.

Landlord's expenses

Once you buy an investment property and become a landlord, there are some expenses you'll regularly have to pay, including:

→ body corporate fees

→ council rates and water

→ interest on your mortgage and bank fees

→ insurance

→ property management fees

→ repairs and maintenance.

The good news is that these expenses are all tax deductible.

Tax talk

When you buy an investment property, you're likely to have plenty of costs that you can claim as a tax deduction at the end of the financial year, including your mortgage interest payments, property management costs, repairs, maintenance and depreciation (among others). Keep all of your paperwork and any receipts for expenses on your investment property to give to your accountant at tax time. They'll let you know what is and isn't deductible.

The bad news is that if you decide to sell an investment property, you'll be required to pay capital gains tax on any profit you make at your marginal tax rate. Again, your accountant will be able to tell you how much tax you're likely to have to pay if you're thinking of selling.

Checklist: buying that property

Decided you'd like to buy property? In a nutshell, here are the basic steps you'll need to follow:

1   *Do your homework.* Buying property is a big commitment, so make sure you cover yourself and do your homework! After you've decided whether the property you plan to buy is going to be a home to live in or an investment property to rent out (as discussed, that's likely to make a big difference to the type of place you buy) check out some of the websites mentioned in this chapter, read *Australian Property Investor* magazine or talk to other people you know who've recently bought property themselves.

2   *Save up for your deposit and enough to cover your purchase costs.* Unless you're extremely cashed up, you're going to need to apply for a loan — most of the big banks have calculators on their website so you can work out how much you might be able to borrow. Aim to save 20 per cent of the purchase price yourself before you approach the banks or other lenders. If you're buying a home to live in and it's your first, you might be eligible for the First Home Owner Grant or the First Home Saver Account. Remember that your costs will include stamp duty (take a deep breath and find out what the damage will be using the calculator on the website of one of the big lenders), bank fees (budget for anywhere between $500 to $1000) and solicitor's fees (expect to pay around $1000).

3   *Protect yourself from a dodgy deal.* If you're negotiating to buy a property, seriously consider including clauses in the contract of sale specifying that your offer is subject to a satisfactory building and pest inspection as well as a satisfactory independent valuation.

If you're going to be buying a property at auction and you're completely in love with it, consider paying for a building and pest inspection to be carried out beforehand. You should already have a realistic idea as to what the property is worth after your extensive research of similar properties in the area and after attending lots of other auctions. Just avoid getting carried away on the day and paying more than you'd planned!

4   *Do your post-purchase paperwork.* If you've bought a home to live in you'll need to make sure it's insured from the day you buy the property, that is, the day you sign the papers — either just after the auction or once you've agreed on a price and finished negotiating with the seller. You'll also need to hire a solicitor to carry out your conveyancing work for you.

If you've bought an investment property to rent out, you'll need to hire a solicitor to carry out your conveyancing work, organise a property manager (if you decide you don't want to manage the property yourself) and take out insurance. You'll also need to arrange for a depreciation report to be carried out as soon as you take possession of the property.

5   *Read away.* There's a lot to learn about buying property successfully. Here are some of the most helpful books available. Knock yourself out!

→   *Real Estate Mistakes* by Neil Jenman (Rowley Publications, 2000)

→   *How to Create an Income for Life* by Margaret Lomas (Wrightbooks, 2007)

→ *Property is a Girl's Best Friend* by Propertywomen.com (Wrightbooks, 2009)

→ *Streets Ahead — How to Make Money from Residential Property* by Monique Wakelin and Richard Wakelin (Wilkinson Publishing, 2007).

Remember: always ask for help if you need it

If you feel you need help — perhaps you'd like to talk to someone who can advise you about how to get a house deposit together — consider seeking the help of a financial adviser. We tell you where you can find one in the 'Help when you need it' section at the back of this book.

part III

extra, extra, read all about it

So, you've reached the third part of your money makeover. By now you've decided on your investment weapon or weapons of choice — shares, managed funds, superannuation or property — and are (hopefully!) eager to plunge yourself into the exciting world of investing.

Before you fly into the home stretch towards financial success there are a few other things you should think about. For example, how you can invest your money in a way that means you won't compromise your personal beliefs or principles? How can you best protect yourself for any unexpected emergencies that might arise? How do you prepare yourself financially for other life events such as shacking up, going back to university or having a baby? By taking these all into consideration now you could be doing yourself a huge favour in years to come. In the next four chapters you'll learn how to:

$ invest responsibly

$ protect yourself with the appropriate insurance

$ navigate your way through the murky waters of money and relationships

$ prepare yourself for the curve balls that life might throw at you (such as going back to further study or having a baby).

chapter 9

responsible
investment

There once was a girl called Irene
Who dreamt of a world pure and clean
She did lots of study
On where to put her money
And now happily invests green.

Do you want to put your hard-earned cash to work in an investment that could make you a lot of money? And do you want to make the world a better place while you're at it? If your answer to these two questions is a resounding 'yes', then responsible investing is for you. It's is all about putting your money to work in investments that give you a warm, fuzzy feeling while potentially making you a healthy return. Responsible investing isn't merely about doing 'the right thing'; it's been proven to be good for your hip pocket. Read on to see why it just might be the smart way to go.

In this chapter we'll cover:

- $ responsible investment 101: what exactly is it?
- $ ethical issues: what's important to you?
- $ finding responsible investments: where do you start?
- $ charitable giving: becoming a philanthropist.

Responsible investment 101: what exactly is it?

While conventional investing is all about the bottom line and typically focuses on how much profit can be made (to the exclusion of just about everything else), responsible investing takes into account environmental, social, ethical or corporate governance considerations as a part of the over-all investment process.

You might be under the impression that becoming a respon-sible investor requires you to start drinking soy chai lattes or drop out of society to live in a commune in the bush. This is definitely not the case. Becoming a responsible investor isn't about trying to achieve sainthood, becoming a hippy or undermining capitalism (but please feel free to try any of these if they take your fancy), although feeling good about the money you're making is certainly a nice side benefit. It's about accepting that you have the power to choose where your money goes and what it finances, not just as a consumer but also as an investor.

Huh?

Responsible investment

In your travels through finance land, you'll probably come across some of the following terms:

→ ethical
→ sustainable
→ green
→ socially responsible.

Don't be confused; they all mean the same thing: responsible investing.

There are lots of everyday investors out there who've made a conscious decision to invest their money responsibly. There are also plenty of multinational companies who are coming to the party and listening to investors who are demanding safer, cleaner production processes and better products. Many of them are actually doing something about it, too — not only to remain competitive, but to maintain their sustainability and increase their profits into the future. More and more financial institutions now offer responsible investment products, such as managed funds and superannuation funds, in order to get a slice of what's becoming an increasing large and lucrative pie.

A study commissioned by the Responsible Investment Association Australasia showed that responsible investment managed funds ran neck and neck (in the Australian shares category) and outperformed (in the overseas shares and balanced growth categories) the average mainstream fund over all time periods up to seven years to June 2009. What does this mean for you? In a nutshell, it's proof that you don't have to compromise your beliefs in order to make a profit.

Ethical issues: what's important to you?

There are a few things you need to know when you start on the path to becoming a responsible investor. You should understand how responsible investments differ from one another (they're not all the same) and you'll need to clarify what issues are important to you.

Approaches to responsible investment

Typically, individuals and financial institutions who want to invest responsibly use one of the following methods:

$ *Negative screening of companies or sectors*. This is where you work out what sort of companies and industries you want to avoid. For example, you might choose to avoid investing in companies that profit from armaments, mine uranium or are involved in animal testing.

$ *Positive investment in sustainable industries.* This is a more proactive type of investment style where you actively seek out companies or industries that have a positive impact on the things you believe in. For example, you might choose to invest in companies that specialise in renewable energy, community banking or organic farming.

What's important to you?

Before you start investing you'll need to clarify the issues that are important to you and decide which companies or industries you want to avoid. Some commonly avoided companies are those that make a profit from:

$ alcohol production or distribution

$ animal welfare abuses

$ armament production or distribution

$ deforestation

$ gaming

$ human rights abuses

$ mining

$ nuclear power

$ tobacco production and distribution.

Next, you should apply your own 'screen' to different investments (whether they're shares, managed funds or superannuation funds) based on what's important to you. For example, you might investigate the activities of any mining company you're considering buying shares in if you're opposed to the development of nuclear power and therefore object to the mining of uranium. Or if you're investing in a managed fund or a superannuation fund, do your research and find out where the fund's money is invested — check out the fund manager's website for details or get yourself a prospectus. Go back and read chapters 5, 6 and 7 of this book if you need a refresher course on investing in shares, managed funds or superannuation.

You'll probably find that choosing a responsible investment is not always clear cut; all you can do is research and choose those companies or funds that most closely match your investment goals and ethical profile.

Huh?

Light green versus dark green

You might hear responsible investment products (managed funds or superannuation funds) being referred to as 'light green' or 'dark green'. This just refers to the investment style that's been applied to that particular fund. Light green funds are typically managed using a negative screening process, while dark green funds often following a more positive investment style (investing in sustainable industries, for example) and are known for applying the strictest screening criteria to their investment portfolio.

Where the smart money is going

Investing responsibly gives you a chance to invest in innovative companies and industries that may well thrive given current (and predicted future) world trends. Imagine if your grandparents or parents had been smart enough to invest in General Electric or Westinghouse back in the 1950s and 1960s, when there was a huge, growing demand for electrical appliances and white goods? Or if they'd looked to the future and invested in Microsoft, Intel or Apple back in the 1980s? By researching and using your smarts this could be *your* chance.

One of the keys to being a successful responsible investor is to stay informed about local and world events. Watch the news, read the papers and keep abreast of what's happening out there, tuning in to any opportunities that might present themselves.

Be aware that the specific issues that matter to you now might change at some point and this will affect your investment decisions. As obvious as it sounds, keep an eye on your investments; you want to make sure that the companies you're investing in now stay aligned with your goals.

Psst ...

The next big thing

When you're thinking about how you're going to invest your money and what industries you might like to support (not to mention those that you think might take off) consider adding these to your list:

→ aged care

→ education

→ health care

→ mass transport

→ microfinance

→ renewable energy and energy efficiency

→ sustainable agriculture

→ sustainable forestry and fishing

→ sustainable property

→ water and waste management.

Keep your eyes peeled—read the news and stay informed.

Finding responsible investments: where do you start?

The first step to becoming a responsible investor is to ensure you have a firm grasp on whatever type of investment has taken your fancy (cash, shares, managed funds, superannuation or property).

Microfinance

The term 'microfinance' refers to the practice of providing credit and other financial services to people in poor communities around the world who've traditionally not had any access to banks, in an attempt to alleviate poverty. Microfinance is a fascinating concept that has its supporters and detractors. If you'd like to find out more, start by reading about Professor Muhammad Yunus and the Grameen Bank in Bangladesh, joint winners of the Nobel Peace Prize in 2006. If you're interested in getting involved directly you can do so through organisations, such as *Kiva*, who organise loans between lenders (people like you) and entrepreneurs in poor communities: <www.kiva.org>.

Once you feel confident you understand the mechanics of these, you'll need to do some extra research in order to invest responsibly. Luckily there are some excellent resources available that will help cut your workload down considerably. Here are five of the best:

1   *The Equator Principles:* a set of guidelines developed in 2003 by a group of some of the world's largest banks to address the social and environmental impacts of the projects they finance across all industry sectors including mining, oil, gas and forestry. Banks that adopt the principles are committed to refusing loans to borrowers that are unable to comply with certain social and environmental policies. Have a look at the website to check out if your bank has signed and is playing ball: <www.equator-principles.com>.

2   *Ethical Investor:* a great website and magazine featuring news of the latest developments in responsible investment and corporate social responsibility. It's very helpful if you're interested in buying shares on the Australian stock market, providing tables with ratings

by Corporate Monitor (a corporate watchdog) on 250 major listed public companies in Australia. It also provides a detailed analysis of responsible managed funds and superannuation funds, including performance stats (data supplied by Morningstar). You have to pay to access this information by subscribing to either the website or the magazine — you'll find full details on the Ethical Investor website. You can also sign up for a free e-newsletter: <www.ethicalinvestor.com.au>.

3   *Google:* yes, good old Google. Do your own research and Google any company (or financial institution) in which you might be thinking of investing. You never know what you might find: <www.google.com.au>.

4   *The Responsible Investment Association Australasia (RIAA):* the peak industry body for professionals working in responsible investment in Australia and New Zealand. It also helps people to learn more about how they can invest responsibly. If you need a point in the right direction, start by looking at the RIAA website. It's a great resource with lots of information for the average punter. It includes lists of co-operative banks and credit unions, fund managers and superannuation fund managers who all follow the principles of responsible investment and provides information about the products they offer: <www.responsibleinvestment.org>.

5   *The United Nations Principles for Responsible Investment (UNPRI):* these were developed by the United Nations with a group of the world's largest institutional investors (fund managers and the like) in 2006 to provide a framework for investment professionals that takes environmental, social and corporate governance issues into consideration when building investment portfolios. In 2009 the UNPRI had 87 Australian signatories, including AustralianSuper and CareSuper. To see the full list take a look at the UNPRI website. It also includes links to interesting articles about responsible investment: <www.unpri.org>.

Ask the hard questions

Lastly, if you can't find any information about your bank or financial institution's own investment policies, don't be afraid to contact them to find out where they stand. If you're investing in shares directly remember that as a shareholder you can have your say about a company's conduct by voting at shareholder meetings. Become involved and don't ever forget that as an investor you have the power to demand positive change.

Nicolette's story (age 36)

When I originally started investing I'd always tried to do so ethically. However after I started writing for *Ethical Investor* magazine I decided I should reorganise my investments along much more specific ethical lines and make sure it was done properly and thoroughly.

I already had a financial adviser whom I trusted and, while he wasn't a specialist in ethical investment, he agreed to look into it. Once we'd established roughly what I considered ethical he was able to go and do the groundwork looking for investments that would suit my needs and meet my expectations.

I ended up investing in ethically managed funds and superannuation (my aim is to invest all of my money ethically). However I've had to be careful—some so-called 'ethical' funds have a clause that allows them to invest in companies that run up to 5 per cent of their business in 'unethical' business areas. The point is that you need to work out what 'ethical' means to you and what level of ethical investing you're aiming for.

Ethical investing is important to me because if I'm not prepared to put in the effort, how could I expect anyone else to?

My advice to anyone who wants to invest ethically: make sure you have a good understanding of what you're doing and what you want to get out of it—and get good advice. It might cost you more in the short term, but it's worth it knowing you're being given the right advice for your situation. Investing ethically is a great thing to do.

Remember: always ask for help if you need it

If you don't feel confident going through the whole process on your own you should see a licensed financial adviser who specialises in responsible investment products. We tell you where you can find one in the 'Help when you need it' section at the back of this book.

Charitable giving: becoming a philanthropist

By now you should be well aware that you don't have to be rich to be an investor — that in fact it's the other way around and you have to be an investor to be rich. Similarly, you don't have to be wealthy to be a philanthropist.

In spite of what we might like to believe about ourselves, by world standards Australians are not a particularly generous bunch. In the United States, charitable giving is around 2.2 per cent of gross national income, which is almost four times as much as charitable giving by Australians. When it comes to volunteering, Australians aren't much better, ranking 11th on the list, well behind the US. When financial donations and volunteering are combined, Australia only manages to squeak in at 16th place on the generosity scale. Considering we're such a wealthy country with one of the highest standards of living in the world, this suggests there's a lot of room for improvement. The question is, how much should we each aim to give? What is a reasonable amount?

Huh?

Philanthropy

Philanthropists are very nice people who give money to charitable causes, often receiving a tax break in the process (more about that later).

World-renowned Australian philosopher Peter Singer (who regularly grapples with heavyweight topics) suggests a sliding scale for giving, based on annual income. His theory is that the more you earn the easier it should be to give — not only in terms of dollars but as a percentage of income. He suggests that Australians of average means should aim to donate 5 per cent of their gross income (that is, income before tax) while the super rich (who earn over $10 million per annum) should aim to donate 33.33 per cent.

In other words, if you currently earn $50 000 per annum he is suggesting you would donate $2500 to charity this year. It might sound like a lot, and it might not be possible if you have a family to support, but it's definitely food for thought. Think about factoring your charitable giving (whatever amount you can afford) into your budget from the get-go. Remember, no matter what your income, you can make a difference — even just a small change in the habits of Australians could go a long way in helping to solve the world's problems.

Peter Singer

If you're interested in reading more about Peter Singer's ideas, check out his book *The Life You Can Save* (Text Publishing, 2009) or his website <www.thelifeyoucansave.com>.

Tax talk

Any donations you make to approved organisations (including those in Australia and overseas) are tax deductible, which will make charitable giving easier on your hip pocket. Your receipt will usually indicate whether or not you can claim a tax deduction for the gift — if you're not sure, you should check with the organisation or with the ATO <www.ato.gov.au>. Make sure you hold on to your receipt as a record come tax time.

chapter 10

insurance

There once was a model named Claire
Whose golden locks caused men to stare
A romantic evening she had
But the candles proved bad
Oh, if only she'd insured her long hair!

Sorting out insurance is one of those important steps that is sometimes overlooked when people start getting their finances in order. Not only is it fairly high up on the yawn-o-meter, but it's not very pleasant to think about worst-case scenarios.

The truth is it's not that hard to sort your insurance situation out — you just need to work out what suits your particular circumstances. Do some online research and you're pretty much there. If you take out the right type of insurance now, you could potentially save yourself a lot of money and keep yourself afloat in the case of an emergency. Plus, being properly insured has the power to give you peace of mind, and that's a pretty nice feeling! In this chapter we'll cover:

$ insurance 101: insurance in a nutshell

- $ insuring yourself and your livelihood: health, income protection, life and travel insurance

- $ insuring your property: house and contents, renter's, landlord's, car and pet insurance

- $ writing a will: protecting your loved ones.

Insurance 101: insurance in a nutshell

You'll find there's insurance to cover pretty much everything these days. There's health, income protection, life and travel insurance (all types of personal insurance) and house and contents, renter's, landlord's and car insurance (all types of property insurance). You can even take out pet insurance to cover your furry friends!

Where to start

It's pretty simple really—decide what's important to you and what you think you need to insure (according to your specific circumstances); do your research by having a look at the policies of a number of insurers who specialise in that type of insurance; and then take out the appropriate cover.

After that, you really only have to worry about updating your insurance policies if your circumstances change. If an insurer makes changes to your policy they have an obligation to contact you to let you know. Maintaining your policy should be as easy as reading your yearly statement and paying the policy renewal.

We'll walk you through each type of insurance in a minute. Some are quite simple and you can easily DIY, but others are more complicated and you might find you need the help of an insurance broker (yes, they do exist) to make sure you take out the right cover. It's imperative that you take out the appropriate type of cover and the right policy to suit your specific circumstances.

Do your homework

No matter what type of insurance you're after, start by perusing the internet. All of the big insurers in Australia are online, so you'll be able to see what types of insurance they offer and in many cases receive a free, no-obligation online quote. This makes it nice and easy to compare different policies. If it takes your fancy you can even buy some policies online — if so, insurers will often give you a discount on your premium (the amount you pay for an insurance policy) for doing so.

Here are some of the big, best-known insurers in Australia. Keep in mind that they won't all offer every type of insurance, but they're a good place to start looking and comparing policies:

$ AAMI: <www.aami.com.au>

$ Allianz Australia: <www.allianz.com.au>

$ Australian Unity: <www.australianunity.com.au>

$ CGU: <www.cgu.com.au>

$ GIO: <www.gio.com.au>

$ HBA: <www.hba.com.au>

$ MBF: <www.mbf.com.au>

$ Medibank Private: <www.medibank.com.au>

$ nib: <www.nib.com.au>

$ QBE Australia: <www.qbe.com.au>.

There are also a number of websites that compare the policies offered by different insurers — very helpful when you're starting to suss out what's available and at what cost. Be warned: some of these sites only compare and provide recommendations on the policies selected by a group of participating insurers — not all of the policies available on the market. However, they should still give you a bit of an idea as to what's out there and at around what price. Consider these:

$ <www.insurancewatch.com.au>: compare income protection and life insurance policies

$ <www.iselect.com.au>: compare health, life and car insurance policies

$ <www.ratecity.com.au>: compare car insurance policies

$ <www.ratedetective.com.au>: compare income protection, life and travel insurance policies

$ CHOICE Online <www.choice.com.au>: the self-proclaimed 'consumer's champion' is another great resource if you want unbiased comparisons on insurance policies. Be warned, you'll have to pay for any reports you download or to subscribe to the site.

You'll also pick up good tips about buying insurance from ASIC's consumer website, FIDO — just type 'insurance' into the search box: <www.fido.gov.au>.

Three important things to remember before you take out insurance

Time to get out the magnifying glass, roll up your shirt sleeves and start reading the fine print. Sure, it's about as fun as doing your tax return but it's vitally important when you're taking out insurance. Here are three things to keep in mind before signing on the dotted line:

1   *Conduct your own thorough research before you sign up with any insurer.* You should compare the policies offered by different insurers (exactly what they cover you for and any conditions they impose) and the price (insurers can charge significantly different amounts for similar types of insurance).

2   *Read any insurance policy very carefully before signing.* You should know exactly what you're getting for your money. Before signing, ask the following questions:

→ What are the exclusions of the policy?

→ Is there an excess (that is, a set amount of money you have to pay whenever you make a claim)?

→ Is there a waiting period before you'll receive any benefits?

If you don't know the answers to these questions or if you don't fully understand the policy make sure you ask either the insurer or your insurance broker.

3 *Provide insurers with the correct details when you're signing up.* Let your insurance company know from the outset if you have any information that might affect your policy or any potential claim that you might make on it in the future. For example, if you're taking out health insurance the insurer will probably ask you to disclose any pre-existing medical conditions you might have. Whatever you do, don't lie to an insurer or withhold information. If they find out, your policy could be voided or, even worse, you could be faced with legal action.

Psst ...

Avoid doubling up on your insurance

Some types of insurance can overlap (for example trauma insurance and life insurance) so read every insurance policy very carefully before signing. This is an easy way of keeping your insurance costs down.

Warning: insurance can be expensive

Yes, some insurance policies can be expensive, but it's important to remember that you really do get what you pay for when insurance is concerned. This is certainly the case with health insurance, where you'll be given the choice of taking out a basic policy that costs the least and covers you for the bare minimum (for example, basic hospital cover only), or a deluxe policy that costs a lot more but has all the bells and whistles (including cover for extras like dental and physiotherapy). You'll need to decide if it's worth your while to pay the extra if you think you might need it, but obviously there's no point in paying for cover that you're unlikely to use.

Psst ...

Want to buy insurance?

Remember Ned Ryerson, that enthusiastic insurance salesman from the movie *Groundhog Day*? If you imagine that all insurance salesman (now known as insurance brokers) fall under a similar guise as Ned, think again. Insurance brokers are helpful people who'll translate tricky insurance-speak and find the right policy for you. It's still a good idea to go in with your eyes open after having done your own research first, and make sure you ask the insurance broker to disclose any commissions they might receive from insurers before you choose one policy over another. We tell you where you can find a licensed insurance broker in the 'Help when you need it' section at the back of this book.

Insuring yourself and your livelihood: health, income protection, life and travel insurance

Most people are quick to take out insurance for their car or other possessions but, strangely, are less likely to insure the most important 'asset' they have — themselves! Here are the main types of personal insurance you should consider.

Health insurance

Picture this: you didn't ever imagine it'd happen to you, but before you can say, 'Don't worry about a condom tonight, it should be okay', you discover you're up the duff. Fortunately, you've got health insurance and can now book yourself into that fancy private hospital with your favourite doctor to look after you.

What is health insurance? Depending on the level of cover provided by the policy, health insurance will help you to pay medical bills, give you access to private hospitals and the doctor of your choice and reduce waiting periods for elective surgery.

Who needs it? There are some enticing reasons to take out health insurance if you're a higher income earner (so earn over $73 000 as a single or over $146 000 as a couple) and don't have health insurance: you won't have to pay the federal government's 1 per cent Medicare Levy Surcharge, and you'll also escape the federal government penalties that kick in after the age of 30 if you don't cover yourself. However, if you're young and healthy or you don't earn a fortune, these might not be compelling enough reasons to sign up — it's up to you to decide.

Ambulance membership

Ambulance costs (which can be very high, even just for a short trip) are not covered by Medicare. If you're a resident of Queensland or Tasmania, you don't have to worry about this because local government taxes pay for ambulance cover. If you live anywhere else in Australia you'll need to cover yourself. If you have health insurance check with your provider to find out exactly what you're covered for — not all health insurers include comprehensive ambulance insurance in their policies. If you don't have health insurance you should think about taking out ambulance membership with your state or territory ambulance service (if they offer it) or take out 'ambulance only' cover with a private health insurer.

Look out for: cheaper health insurance policies that don't cover your unique circumstances. Like most things, you get what you pay for and you'll probably find that a basic health insurance policy won't cover the cost of your Pilates classes or Kahuna massage sessions (if you were expecting it to). Just read the fine print so you don't get any nasty surprises come claim time.

Income protection insurance

Picture this: you didn't think your boyfriend's idea to spend the weekend skiing at Mt Hotham was a particularly great one given your pre-existing medical condition: two left feet. No one could ever accuse you of not having a go, however, and now you're laid up in hospital with broken bones, unable to move (let alone work) for eight months. While some of your time out will be covered by sick leave, it was fortunate you'd taken out income protection insurance so you'll have a regular income coming in for the rest of the time you're on your back — literally.

What is income protection insurance? This kind of insurance will provide you with an ongoing income (usually up to 75 per cent of your current income) in the event that you're injured or become ill and cannot work. Note that it won't cover you if you're made redundant or if you're fired from your job! The good news is that premiums are tax deductible.

Who needs it? Anyone who works to support themselves or their dependents (if they have them) should be covered by income protection insurance. Just think, how would you survive if you were unable to work — who'd support you and your family? Primary caregivers should also be covered — if you're a stay-at-home mum or dad just think, who'd look after your little ones if you were unable to?

Look out for: tricky clauses hidden in the fine print. Some of the most common ones are:

$ *The waiting period.* How long after you've become incapacitated before you'll start to receive payments? If you choose a short waiting period (say, one month) you'll pay a much higher premium so think carefully about this one. Would you be covered by your employer's sick leave and, if so, for how long? Could you fall back on your emergency savings for a month or two before your insurance kicks in? By choosing a longer waiting period it could reduce your premium substantially.

$ *Usual occupation versus any occupation.* You should take out a policy that covers you in the event that you're unable to work in your 'usual occupation.' If you take out an 'any occupation' policy it means the insurer won't pay you while you're capable of doing *any* job — not so good!

$ *Non-cancellable contracts.* Make sure the policy will cover you for as long as you're unable to work, no matter how long that might be or how often you fall ill.

$ *Indexation of benefits.* In the event that you're unable to work for a long time make sure that your benefits are indexed (that is, that they increase over time, to counter the effects of inflation).

Huh?

Trauma insurance and total and permanent disablement insurance

Just the words 'trauma' and 'total and permanent disablement' are enough to make you grimace and turn the page quickly, but you will come across them — so keep reading! Not exactly income protection insurance or life insurance but somewhere in-between, trauma insurance will cover you with a lump-sum payment should you be diagnosed with a major listed illness or disease and total and permanent disablement insurance will cover you with a lump-sum payment if you become totally and permanently disabled. These policies are usually offered alongside income protection and life insurance policies—if you decided to take out either one just make sure you're not doubling up and covering yourself for the same thing twice.

Income protection insurance is pretty complicated, so see a licensed financial adviser or insurance broker if you feel you need help.

Life insurance

Picture this: you're sitting up at the pearly gates with The Big Guy. While you're a bit dazed and confused (what were the chances of that asteroid falling where it did?) you're relieved you took out life insurance last year — at least your loved ones won't need to worry about money.

What is life insurance? Life insurance pays a lump sum to the person you nominate if you die.

Who needs it? Everyone with children or other dependents should have life insurance — and not only the breadwinner of the family. Anyone whose primary responsibility it is to care for dependents should also be covered by life insurance as that way, if something happens to them, the remaining partner will be able to afford to pay for help while they work. You could also take out life insurance if you don't have dependents, but if you have debt (perhaps a home loan) and would like it to be cleared in the event of your death.

Look out for: complicated policies. Speak to a licensed financial adviser or insurance broker if you'd like help sorting it out. Be aware that your superannuation fund might include some life insurance however it could be quite minimal, so check on this before deciding that you don't need to take out a separate life insurance policy.

Travel insurance

Picture this: you're overseas and far away from home, and you've woken up with a nasty rash, never mind where. It's probably not life threatening, but it's worrying (not to mention itchy) and you'd like to get to a doctor to have it checked out, pronto. Fortunately, you'd taken out travel insurance which will cover your medical costs — and now you can spend your hard-earned cash on more important things ... like German beer halls for example.

What is travel insurance? It covers you for a range of events such as cancellation of your holiday, illness, loss of your possessions and personal liability (if you injure someone or something while you're travelling).

Who needs it? Anyone travelling overseas for any length of time should take out travel insurance without fail!

Look out for: clauses that don't cover your specific circumstances. For example, you might not be covered if you were to participate in any 'dangerous activities' such as heli-skiing or travel in a country that had a travel warning.

Travel insurance online

While it's easy and convenient to organise travel insurance through your travel agent, don't be lazy and be sure to check what else is out there before you sign up—you might find something cheaper online or through one of the 'traditional' big insurers.

Samantha's story (age 32)

Three years ago I decided I wanted a change of scene, so I applied for a Canadian working visa. Pretty soon I was packing my bags and heading to Whistler, to work as a ski instructor for a year.

After my year was up, I decided to stay in Canada for another couple of weeks before heading for home. I took out travel insurance to cover myself for the remainder of my stay. Problem was, I didn't read the fine print—and that's where I got myself into trouble. I went out skiing with a friend, and while we were exploring the mountain we decided to head off-piste (that is, off the marked runs). It was pretty steep and even though I'm a good skier I took a really bad turn, falling for a couple of hundred metres down an

Samantha's story (cont'd)

icy slope. In the process I concussed myself, broke several ribs, my collar bone and one of my legs.

I had to be airlifted off the mountain to a hospital in Vancouver, and then home to Australia on a full stretcher on a Qantas flight. While I was very lucky not to have been permanently injured, I didn't get away with it scot free: my accident ended up costing around A$180 000, and here's the kicker: my travel insurance didn't cover *any* of the cost (not even the hospital bills) because I'd been skiing off the marked runs. My parents had to re-mortgage their house to pay the bills, and while I'm slowly paying them back it's going to take years to get rid of my debt.

My advice to anyone travelling overseas is to make sure your travel insurance covers you for any activities you might be planning, especially if it's anything that could be considered dangerous (including extreme sports)! Always read the fine print.

Insuring your property: house and contents, renter's, landlord's, car and pet insurance

Now it's time to think about insuring your possessions. Read on to learn all about insuring everything from your true love (your Monaro) to your furry friend Sam the Schnauzer.

House and contents insurance

Picture this: you've just arrived home from a weekend down at the beach only to discover that the charming display of thunder and lightning over the city you enjoyed last night from a distance had resulted in a river of water flowing down one side of your house and through your lounge room. Fortunately, you'd taken out house and contents insurance, which will cover the cost of repairs, including a new carpet, lounge suite and television.

What is home and contents insurance? Home insurance covers your home, garage and any other buildings, walls, gates, fences and driveways you own. Experts recommend that you have replacement cover (that is, cover that will buy you a brand new fence, for example, despite the fact that the cost of fencing might have increased since you took out your policy) for all items and provision for the full cost of rebuilding in the event of major catastrophe. Contents insurance covers the fittings inside your home such as carpets and curtains, as well as your personal possessions, for damage or theft. Always get expensive items such as jewellery and antiques valued separately — you may need specific cover for these items. Note: if you live in an apartment or unit with a body corporate, the building will be covered by their insurance. You should still take out contents insurance to cover the fittings inside your own apartment and your personal possessions.

Who needs it? Anyone who owns their own home needs house and contents insurance. If you're renting, we'll get to you next — you'll need renter's insurance instead.

Look out for: underinsuring. Most people underinsure out of ignorance or to avoid having to pay a higher premium, but this really is counterproductive. Always make sure that you cover your house and contents for their full replacement value. If you're unsure your insurer should be able to give you some guidelines (based on how big your house is and what it's made of, for example) or you can pay a professional valuer to put a price on your home and contents for you. Many insurance company websites list professional valuers and their contact details.

Renter's insurance

Picture this: *you thought he looked a bit dodgy but you just didn't have the heart to tell your flatmate she should think twice about her choice of new boyfriend. When things start to go missing and you then spot* *his mug on Crime Stoppers, it all falls into place — but not before he's nicked off with half of your stuff. Fortunately, you'd taken out renter's insurance which will cover you for the items that have been stolen.*

What is renter's insurance? It will cover your possessions in the case of theft, fire or any number of other unfortunate incidents. What's covered will vary from insurer to insurer, so make sure you check.

Who needs it? If you're renting or living in share accommodation renter's insurance is for you — especially if you own possessions that are particularly valuable. You can generally organise renter's insurance on your own, as insurers will often allow for multiple separate policies per household. This means you won't have to wait for your flatmates to get themselves sorted out before you can get yourself covered.

Look out for: any thrash metal band members who might want to rent one of the rooms in your place. Also, make sure that you don't underinsure. Again, it's important that you cover your possessions adequately so have a good stab at working out what it would cost to replace them.

Renter's insurers

Not all of the big insurers offer renter's insurance, however here are some that do:

→ AAMI or NRMA Insurance (if you're in ACT, NSW, QLD or TAS)

→ RACV (if you're in VIC)

→ SGIC (if you're in SA)

→ SGIO (if you're in WA).

Landlord's insurance

Picture this: your new tenants seemed great on paper, but it turns out their rental application was full of holes — and now your walls are, too. Not only have they trashed the place, but they've absconded, owing you two month's rent. Fortunately, you'd taken out landlord's insurance so you're covered for the cost of repairs, rent default and loss of rent (if it takes a while before you find new tenants).

What is landlord's insurance? This type of insurance specifically covers investment property for loss or damage to building or contents, public liability (in case anyone is injured on your property), damage, theft and rent default by tenants and loss of rent. The good news is that it's tax deductible.

Who needs it? You should definitely take out landlord's insurance if you own an investment property that's being rented for residential purposes.

Look out for: hefty excesses. Make sure you check how much you'll have to pay towards any claim you might have to make (this is called the 'excess'). Some insurers charge much higher excesses than others and this could really eat into any payment you might receive.

Car insurance

Picture this: *it was early morning, foggy, and a light rain had been falling, so the road was wet. You weren't driving very fast but all of a sudden your neighbour's kamikaze moggy jumped out in front of you and you swerved, ploughing your beautiful new Subaru Outback into an oncoming car. Luckily, no-one was hurt, but neither car came off particularly well and the repair bills are obviously going to run into the thousands. Fortunately, you'd taken out comprehensive car insurance which will pay for repairs to both cars (although it won't cover the vet's bills once you get your hands on that cat ...).*

What is car insurance? It protects you and other drivers in the event of an accident. There are three main types:

1   *Compulsory third party.* Mandatory when you register your car — it covers claims made against you by someone you injure while driving as well as your legal costs, but not the cost of repairs to your own or anyone else's car.

2   *Third party property.* Covers you for damage caused by your car to property owned by a third party. It doesn't cover the cost of repairs to your own car, however if you take out what's called *third party fire and theft* you're covered if your car is damaged by (surprisingly) fire or through theft.

3   *Comprehensive.* Premiums for comprehensive car insurance can be pricey, however this is the type of cover with all the bells and whistles. You'll be covered for any damage you may cause to the property of anyone else as well as any damage to your own car — even if you're at fault.

Who needs it? Car insurance is important for anyone who owns and drives a car. Compulsory third party insurance is just that — compulsory (for all car owners), however you should consider taking out a higher level of cover if you can afford it, especially if you drive a nice car (or if, deep down, you know you're a bad driver).

Look out for: Volvo drivers — urban myth perhaps, but give them a wide berth whenever possible, just in case they live up to their reputation.

Specialist car insurers

You might notice ads out there for Bingle <www.bingle.com.au> and Just Car Insurance <www.justcarinsurance.com.au>. They are both underwritten by AAMI — it's not a trick, just a bit of a marketing ploy to offer a slightly different product to different customers.

Emergency roadside assistance

You should also consider taking out emergency roadside assistance in the event that your car breaks down on the road (although you can usually do this on the spot, which is great if you don't get around to it but then find yourself broken down on a dark road one night). It's not too expensive — contact your state or territory motoring association for details. They all offer car insurance too, and you can get quotes online.

Pet insurance

Picture this: Your best friend Bertie the Beagle hadn't been looking too good, and, after an X-ray and a rather uncomfortable-looking internal examination by the local vet, you discover he's swallowed a golf ball (whole) which is only going to cost $3000 to remove. Fortunately, you've taken out pet insurance so you're not going to have to sell your granny to pay for it.

What is pet insurance? It covers vet and surgery fees in the event that your pet is injured in an accident or becomes ill. Policies usually cover dogs, cats and horses, but check with individual insurers.

Who needs it? Good for anyone who's the proud owner of a dog, cat or horse — particularly if your pet is adventurous and/ or likely to do (or eat) something silly.

Look out for: golf courses. Don't let Bertie near one again!

Pet insurers

If you're interested in taking out pet insurance to cover your furry friend try PetSure (Australia) <www.petsure.com.au> or Petplan Australia <www.petplan.com.au>.

Writing a will: protecting your loved ones

A will is a legal document that states who you want to inherit your assets after your death and names a guardian for your children if you have any. If you die without a will, your estate will be divided up by a court who'll decide who gets what — and it won't necessarily be divided up the way you might like it. So every adult should have a current will.

You should make sure you update your will whenever your circumstances change—if, for example, you get married, enter into a de facto relationship, get divorced, have children or if the death of a relative, friend or anyone else affects your current will. You've got two options when it comes to preparing a will: doing it yourself, or employing a solicitor to draw up your will on your behalf. Here are the details of each option:

1   *See a solicitor.* You can pay a solicitor to write up a will for you. It's definitely a good idea to see a solicitor if you feel that you need help with this, especially if your affairs are more complicated. As a rough guide, a solicitor should be able to prepare a basic will starting at around $300.

2   *Do it yourself.* If your affairs aren't complex and you'd like to write your will yourself you can buy a do-it-yourself legal will kit. They're usually available from your local newsagent or bookseller or you can go online and buy one from Legal Wills Made Easy: <www.legalwills.com.au>. If you think your situation is a bit tricky or if you're unsure if you're up to the task, you should definitely pay a solicitor to write up a will for you.

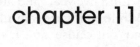

chapter 11

love and money

There once was a girl called Leanne
Who hid her new dress from her man
Things suddenly turned bleak
When he discovered the receipt
Till she found he'd just splurged on a van.

If only getting your finances on track was as simple as sorting out your own affairs. Sigh. As soon as you add another person into the picture, things start to become a little more complicated.

Money is a very powerful factor in relationships—it determines how you live, where you live and, ultimately, your future. But it's rare that two people have exactly the same idea about managing money, and unfortunately fancying the pants off each other isn't going to be enough to see you through. Money is also a mighty hard topic to talk about—it's up there with discussing the ex in the awkward-subject-matter stakes.

It's vital to get things off on the right track from the start, for all sorts of reasons. Once the rose tinted glasses come off, you don't want to end up spending your days arguing over the cost of home brand versus organic muesli or whether or not you can afford to take that holiday. You also need to protect yourself — the cold hard facts are that 40 per cent of de facto couples break up within five years and around half of all Australian marriages fail. While it might seem mercenary to enter a relationship that has an 'out clause' attached to it, you do need to be aware of how best to protect your hard earned investments. In this chapter we'll cover:

$ the early days: how to get financially in-tune with your beloved

$ getting serious: powering up your joint investments

$ splitsville: how to protect yourself in a break-up

$ five rules to follow: how to live fiscally-ever-after.

The early days: how to get financially in-tune with your beloved

In the early dating stages, the greatest financial decision you'll probably make is who's paying for what on each date. But when things start getting a bit more serious and you decide to shack up, the money side of things can become tricky.

Almost three quarters of couples now employ the 'try before you buy' philosophy and live together before tying the knot, or choose not to tie the knot at all. Moving in is exciting and can be oh-so-romantic to begin with ... those shared candle-lit dinners gazing at each other across the dinner table, trips to Ikea for homewares and your first joint purchase. But as any relationship veteran will tell you, those heady early days do eventually morph into toilet seats being left up, wet towels being left on the floor and discoveries of dirty magazines under the mattress.

Shacking up

If you're about to join the 1.5 million or so Australians who live together as de facto couples, brace yourself for the adjustment phase of changing your 'I' to a 'we.'

You'll go from having your own money to spend as you choose to joint bills and purchases and a degree of accountability to someone else. This can be hard if you have different spending habits, earn different amounts of money or if you have different financial goals. While perhaps a bit tricky, managing your finances as a couple certainly doesn't have to be impossible. On the contrary, living with someone else can have great financial advantages: two people can live more cheaply than one; you have double the resources behind you; and you have someone else to keep you motivated and on track to reach any financial goals you set together.

The key to a successful money partnership is to have an understanding of where the other person is coming from, to share goals (and put systems in place to achieve them) and to treat each other equally in all financial decisions. We'll now discuss each of these in detail.

Communicate

Money can be seen as a bit of a grubby subject and can be difficult to bring up in conversation. In fact, a 2006 survey by the Financial Services Authority in the UK revealed that three quarters of couples found it the hardest topic to talk about. Interestingly, the same survey also found that men would do anything to avoid talking about finance, with one third of them preferring to answer questions about their partners' personal appearance — yikes! Despite this, it's vital to take a deep breath and bring it up with your partner early on. If they're reluctant to engage on the subject, you'll need to try to work out a strategy to get them to discuss it. Try to understand each other's attitudes to money as well as your own habits and expectations and keep the lines of communication open at all times. Most importantly, you should agree that no big financial decision should be made without prior discussion — no matter who earns what.

Have a joint vision

Work out how you'd like to approach money as a couple. Think about how you want to live and agree on your goals and priorities. At least then you can be confident you're both working towards achieving the same vision. This doesn't mean you can't have your own separate goals and financial independence; it just means there's a common understanding when it comes to the money you share.

Set up systems

Lay down your financial ground rules from the start. It's all terribly unromantic, but much less so than bickering about money later on. Considerations should include:

§ *What are your joint expenses?* You should start by working out what your joint expenses are likely to be every month (including rent, groceries and utility bills). Try to think of every expense and make sure you agree on exactly what costs you're jointly responsible for paying. For tips on budgeting go back and read chapter 2.

§ *How much will you each pay towards your joint expenses?* This can be a little bit of a grey area, particularly if you earn very different amounts of money. Come to an agreement on whether you'll pay all of your bills 50/50 or come up with another arrangement that might be fairer. One way to work out how to split expenses would be to use the method recommended by American money-relationship-guru Suze Orman. Her philosophy is that each partner pays a set percentage of household expenses every month (including rent) that is based on the amount of money they earn. So, if you earn more you contribute more and vice-versa.

How to split your household expenses à la Suze Orman

Sara brings home $5000 a month. She lives with her boyfriend Josh, who brings home $3000 a month. They calculate what percentage each of them should contribute using the following four steps.

→ *Step one:* add up all shared monthly expenses: $4000 per month.

→ *Step two:* add up combined monthly take home pay: $8000 ($5000 from Sara and $3000 from Josh).

→ *Step three:* work out the percentage of shared monthly expenses to combined monthly take-home pay: $4000 expenses to $8000 take home pay = 50 per cent

→ *Step four:* use this percentage to determine how much each partner contributes each month: Sara pays $2500 (50 per cent of her pay) and Josh pays $1500 (50 per cent of his pay).

§ *Who has bill-payer duties?* You should decide who'll be responsible for paying the rent and bills on time and where the money for this will come from. For example, if you agree to be the bill payer, how (and when) will your partner pay you for their share? Remember, automatic payments are your friend: you could set up a system so that an agreed amount of money is automatically transferred from your partner's account to your account on a particular date each month. That way you'll never have to harass your partner for their share of the money (never much fun).

§ *Will you have a joint fund to pay for joint expenses?* Consider whether you want to set up a joint account to use as a shared pool for household expenses and joint purchases. In this case, you could each contribute an agreed amount from your individual accounts into the shared pool on a set date each month and then the bill-payer would be responsible for paying all bills from this account instead of their own. A word of warning: if you do set up a joint bank account for a shared household pool it does come with some serious considerations — more about that one later.

Other living considerations

Before you call the removalists and start the fun task of working out what furniture goes where, you should fully understand the ins and outs of co-signing a rental lease or co-owning a property together:

§ *Renting*. It's a good idea for both names to be on any lease or rental agreement you sign, because this gives you both equal rights as co-tenants. The biggest advantage of this is that if one of you were to walk out, the remaining partner would have the right to remain as the tenant (although they'd be responsible for covering all of the rent).

§ *Buying*. When buying a property together there are generally two types of co-ownership — tenancy in common and joint tenancy. Tenants in common each own a nominated portion of the property and are only responsible for their share, whereas joint tenants own (and are responsible for) the entire property together. Under both arrangements, it is advised that a co-ownership agreement be arranged outlining each partner's rights and obligations in case of separation, selling the house or buying your partner out. Separately to this, you need to work out how to structure your home loan. It's a good idea to ensure that any home loan you decide to take out together is a joint loan that requires both of your signatures to make any changes. Remember that if one of you defaults on your mortgage repayments, both of you are jointly liable. You can read more about buying property in chapter 8.

Huh?

STDs

We're not talking STDs of the itchy-down-there kind, but rather sexually transmitted debt, now a hugely common and very nasty condition where you can unwittingly end up being responsible for your partner's debt. Commonly, this is when a person signs something to help her partner get a loan (that is, becomes a guarantor or co-borrower) and then finds herself primarily liable for the repayments if her partner leaves town or can't make the payments. Financial STDs should be avoided at all costs — there isn't any ointment that can soothe this sort of pain.

Proceed with caution

If you're considering helping your partner out with a loan, or setting up a bank account or credit card together, you should tread very carefully. 'Be alert but not alarmed', as Johnny H once said! Some things to consider when in this situation:

$ *Co-borrowing.* If your partner asks you to sign any loan documentation, be very careful! If you become a co-borrower or act as guarantor of any loan, you may be liable for paying back half or all of the debt — even if you haven't benefited from borrowing the money yourself. What would happen if you couldn't keep up the repayments? How would this impact on your credit rating? Give serious consideration before agreeing to sign anything — it's your hard-earned money, after all.

$ *Joint bank accounts.* Be very cautious about sharing your savings, particularly in the first few years of your relationship. Consider setting up a joint account for household expenses only, as discussed earlier. If you do set up an account together, it's a great idea to keep your own individual accounts as well. That way you retain your financial independence and avoid the 'Did you really need to buy that?' arguments. Also, avoid opening an account that has an overdraft facility. Remember that if you go the whole hog and start putting all your money into a joint account, it's effectively giving someone else access to all your savings.

$ *Joint credit cards.* Just like opening a joint bank account, you should approach this with extreme caution — especially in the early days of your relationship. If you both decide you want to go this way, make sure you set a realistic credit limit that you know you can pay back each month. Try to agree on the maximum amount you're allowed to spend on any one item (for example $400); any purchase that costs more than that would need to be discussed before the purchase goes ahead. Read more about credit in chapter 2.

Fiscal fibbing

According to a 2005 survey in the US, one third of all adults (men and women) in committed relationships have lied to their partners about the cost of something, with one in four admitting that lying about money worried them more than lying about sex.

Getting serious: powering up your joint investments

In long-term relationships you have the opportunity to power it up in the investment stakes: you now have double the income and double the resources. Not only will your living costs be reduced (sharing the cost of rent, groceries, petrol, etc., is cheaper than paying for them on your own), but there are other advantages to living in the Kingdom of Coupledom. For example, a bank is much more likely to approve you for a home loan when there are two of you to service the loan, rather than one.

Saving towards joint goals

As your 'I' starts to change to 'we', you might want to think about what you want to achieve together (holidays or home deposits, for example) and set some savings goals. How much you're able to save will be affected by any regular personal expenses you might have (gym memberships or guitar lessons, for example), but it helps to set yourself a monthly goal that you can each work towards. You should be realistic as to how much you can regularly save without curtailing your lifestyle — check out chapters 2 and 3 for tips with budgeting and saving. You'll also need to decide where you'd like this money to be invested: do you want to stick with your own everyday transaction accounts, or would you consider setting up a joint online savings account that earns a bit more interest? Work out what suits you both best.

Cassie's story (age 33)

From an early age I've been a great saver. I started part-time work at about the age of 14 and opened a savings account straight away. Since then I've always saved as much as I could—that way, if I want something nice I know I can afford it.

When I moved in with my partner seven years ago, I knew he wasn't great with money so I took over the financial side of things. We set up a system where both salaries would be paid into one account, and then I'd be responsible for paying bills, doling pocket money out to us both and saving the rest.

The biggest adjustment for me was having to consult my partner before buying joint purchases after being financially independent from such a young age. Even though we had the same weekly pocket money, I suddenly found myself buying things and then hiding them, feeling as if I had to justify my spending to someone else. Our priorities on how we spent money were (and still are) completely different. This causes arguments—usually me thinking he's wasting it and him thinking I'm tight!

Cassie's story (cont'd)

Changing someone else's spending habits is a massive challenge, but over the years we've both worked hard to meet somewhere in the middle. My partner now lives within his means and I've learnt to let go a little. Despite our differences we've achieved a lot. We saved enough so that in one year we paid for our dream wedding, the most amazing honeymoon and still had enough left over for a deposit for our first home. What I've learnt is that you both need to be honest from the start about what you want and need from your money. Chances are your habits and outlook will be quite different so it's vital that you both compromise.

Be equally involved

Alarmingly, recent surveys have found that in committed relationships, men are still much more likely to be in charge of investment decisions and retirement savings than women. It cannot be stressed enough how important it is that you take an active role in all investment decisions and totally understand what you and your partner are investing in. Don't *ever* hand over the responsibility of managing your finances to someone else, no matter how much you trust them. There's no law that forces someone to do a good job of managing your money.

Psst ...

Income splitting

If you and your partner earn different amounts and are on different tax rates, it's worth talking to an accountant about whether there are any benefits to investing in one of your names, in order to reduce the overall amount of tax you pay as a couple.

De facto territory — two years and beyond

While you might be breaking out the champagne to celebrate your two-year anniversary, reaching the second-year milestone also marks something a little more serious. You have just hit de facto territory, and this is when all sorts of legal stuff kicks in. Once you're legally defined as a de facto couple, you're pretty much considered the same as a married couple when it comes to dividing up any assets if you break up.

Consider this scenario: let's say you're living in a house that you own (or are paying off), then your partner moves in and pays you rent (which you pay towards the mortgage) or helps you out by renovating or tending the garden. Even if their name is not on the mortgage or property title, if you split up after a considerable length of time together your partner may be able to claim part of your home. Or, if you inherit money from a relative and invest it in a joint asset, your partner doesn't even have to have met the deceased to make a claim on that money. These are extreme examples, but definitely food for thought.

Defining de facto

Under the *Family Law Act 1975*, a de facto relationship is one where two people (who are not married) have been living together as a couple. This means same-sex couples have the same rights as unmarried couples in areas such as tax, property, super and spousal maintenance.

Although there are no hard-and-fast rules, the Family Law Court can order the division of a de facto couple's assets (property, superannuation, etc.) and spousal maintenance if they are satisfied that one of the following is the case:

→ The relationship has lasted over two years in total (in one or several periods).

→ You have children together.

Defining de facto *(cont'd)*

→   One of you has made significant financial or
     non-financial contributions (that is, as a homemaker
     or parent) and there would be a serious injustice
     if a court order were not made.

In making their assessment of whether a couple are de facto, the
court may take into account a range of factors including whether a
sexual relationship existed, the degree of financial interdependence
and how the relationship was viewed by friends. Note that slightly
different criteria exists for couples in Western Australia.

Co-habitation agreements: protect yourself

Before moving in, consider whether or not you should have a
financial agreement drawn up. A financial agreement is a legal
document that lists what assets each of you bring to the relationship and how they will be divided up in the case of separation.
These are commonly called a co-habitation agreement for de facto
couples or a pre-nuptial agreement for married couples — and
they are no longer the domain of the rich and famous.

While it's sure to sober any romantic dinner (you'll need a
few stiff drinks before broaching this one) and you risk seeming
distrustful, it's definitely worth considering — particularly if
you're entering a relationship with more assets than your partner.
At the very least you should find out how the law will regard your
assets in the event of a split. Then you can decide whether or not
you want to protect them. To have a financial agreement drawn
up, you and your partner will need to seek independent financial
and legal advice (see the 'Help when you need it' section at the
back of this book if you need to find a lawyer).

Beware the jilted lover!

Brace yourself: if you take a lover who could be defined as your de facto by the courts and then split up, they may be able to apply for spousal maintenance—that is, financial support from you if they are unable to adequately support themselves. That you're in another relationship, or even if you're married to someone else, is no defence—the same law applies.

Splitsville: how to protect yourself in a break-up

No-one likes to think of worst-case scenarios, but you do need to understand how best to protect yourself in case your relationship doesn't make it. Imagine how terrible it would be to split up and then discover that you have no idea where on earth your money is! This may all appear a bit bleak and pessimistic, and your finances probably aren't going to be on your mind if you're in the early throes of a new relationship, but think of it in the best girl-scout light: while hopefully you'll never need to action this, on the off chance that you do break up, you'll be prepared.

People don't tend to end long-term relationships on the spur-of-the-moment. It's something that's usually considered well in advance, and it's not uncommon for people to start moving money and assets around in anticipation of a break up. While we certainly aren't advocating this (nasty work, if you ask us) you should be aware that it's pretty common. To best prepare yourself financially for a breakup, you should make sure you do the following things:

$ Make sure you know where all of your money is invested, and keep the originals or copies of all of your financial paperwork and documentation.

§ Keep an eye on all joint bank, credit and loan accounts — make sure that money doesn't start going missing and that 'unauthorised' spending doesn't start getting racked up.

§ Employ your own accountant and lawyer if you don't already have them.

If D-Day has arrived, you probably don't feel like doing anything more than watching crappy movies and sobbing into your pillow. But the best thing you can do for your future wellbeing is to haul yourself up and have a look at the following — pronto:

§ *Joint accounts.* What to do here depends on how your accounts have been set up and your personal circumstances. Firstly, you should strongly consider cancelling any joint credit cards or accounts. If this is your only bank account and source of cash, consider setting a limit with the bank where both signatures are required to withdraw anything over a set amount of money. Make sure you have enough money somewhere other than your joint account so that you can live independently for at least the first few months of the break up. You don't want to be left high and dry with no access to your money. If you've moved to a new address, make sure you let your bank and financial institutions know and tell them that you'd like to receive a copy of any future correspondence.

§ *Your own accounts.* Change your password on your own bank accounts and, if it's a bad break-up, make sure it's not something that your ex will guess!

§ *Paperwork.* Make sure you have all of your financial paperwork handy for every investment you own. Secure these somewhere safe.

§ *Seek advice.* Working out what you're entitled to can be a complicated process, particularly if you're unable to come to an agreement with your ex, so be sure to seek advice from a lawyer about your affairs. Interestingly, women often take less than they are entitled to because they can't afford legal fees or want to avoid an ugly drawn-out dispute. Carefully consider your future and think about whether your decision will be something you can happily live with down the track.

$ *Keep the lines of communication open.* The best possible scenario is to end up with a good relationship with your ex, particularly if you have children. To help you achieve this, consider using a family dispute resolution service. Check out Relationships Australia or the Family Mediation Centre. The federal government website is a good place to start: <www.familyrelationships.gov.au>.

Five rules to follow: how to live fiscally-ever-after

Here are five basic money rules to help you live happily ever after (in the financial stakes, at least). They are:

$ *Rule one: talk.* Communication is the key. Make sure you can talk to your partner about all things money, ranging from how much you think you should spend on groceries to how you should invest for your future. It's not a particularly nice topic (talking about your future holiday plans is far more fun!), but it's an essential one for your future financial health. Once you have figured out some strategies for getting your partner to open up (if they're a bit reluctant) you're halfway there. Ensure all major financial decisions are discussed before they're made — remember: you're an equal partnership.

$ *Rule two: agree on goals and systems.* Make sure you both agree on your expectations in terms of spending and saving. Then, set up systems that you can both stick to. An agreed monthly automatic payment from the non-bill paying partner to the bill-paying partner (or from both partners to a joint account if that's the way you decide to go) will make things nice and easy. Once you're set up and the ground rules have been laid out, you'll have the best chance of avoiding problems down the track and you can forget about it and get on with more fun things.

$ *Rule three: power it up.* There are great financial advantages to being part of a couple. Not only will you save on Christmas and wedding presents (unless you've just found yourself part of a family of breeders), but you'll also have double the income and double the brain power to kick some financial goals.

$ *Rule four: know where you stand.* If your relationship is getting serious, make sure you fully understand the financial and legal implications of being in a de facto relationship or marriage. Remember, if you're living with someone for more than two years or have a child with them, you could be viewed by the courts in exactly the same way as a married couple (in terms of your assets, at least). Consider signing a binding financial agreement before you shack up (a co-habitation agreement for a de facto couple or a pre-nuptial agreement for a married couple, for example).

$ *Rule five: look out for number one.* Make sure you always retain your independence and never hand over responsibility for your personal finances to your partner. At the end of the day, you're the one who'll have to live with the consequences of any decisions (good or bad) made about your investments. You should always understand exactly where your money is — after all, it's your life and your hard-earned cash. Plus, as we've already banged on about, as a woman you're better equipped to be a financial guru than men anyway. Always make sure you're involved.

chapter 12

what life
throws at you

There once was a girl called Jane
Who lived with her boyfriend Wayne
They enjoyed roly-poly
But their condom was holey
Now they're a threesome with little Elaine.

Unfortunately for the anally retentive among us, life doesn't always head in a neat linear line from A to Z. While you might make the best-laid plans for your future, who knows what little curve balls may get thrown your way?

Life's little events impact on your finances, both in the short term and the long term. You might decide to go back to university or to head overseas for a stint of work or a long holiday; you might pop out a bubby; or even come into a windfall (lucky duck!). Of course, it's these things that make life rich (in the non-monetary sense) and allow you to live life to the fullest. With a little thought and research you'll be able to minimise the impact of unexpected curve balls on your finances and make the most of opportunities as they come your way. In this chapter we'll cover:

- _S_ adventures: heading overseas for fun and work
- _S_ investing in you: back to school
- _S_ family matters: up the duff
- _S_ windfalls: inheritance and the lottery.

Adventures: heading overseas for fun and work

It's a rite of passage for young Australians to head overseas at some point. Who wouldn't want to spend their limited time on earth exploring all that it offers: the New York skyline, the mouth-watering cuisine of Italy or discovering the lost ruins of Machu Picchu in Peru?

How you attack paying for your travels depends on the sort of trip you're after. Do you want a break from work to spend six months travelling, or do you want to take your career to an international level and work overseas (or perhaps even do both)? Whatever you decide is obviously going to have an impact on your finances.

Happy holidays

If you want to take some time away from the nine-to-five grind and head off on a travelling adventure, there are four financial steps to think about:

1. *Map out your dream trip.* The fun part! Decide where you want to go to and for how long.

2. *Cost out your dream trip.* Work out your set 'before you leave' costs and your variable 'on the ground' holiday costs.

→   *Set costs*: write a list of every cost you can think of — for example airline tickets, accommodation, tours, new backpack, sleeping bag and clothes to suit the local climate. Don't forget to factor in travel insurance. Overseas medical expenses can be *trés* expensive if something happens to you (you can read more about insurance in chapter 10).

→   *Variable costs*: work out roughly how much money you think you'll need each day for things like food, transport and sightseeing. To do this accurately, you'll need to research the basic living costs at each of your destinations. Travel guide books and websites such as <www.tripadvisor.com.au> will be helpful for this.

3   *Put together a savings plan.* Once you've tallied up all your costs, you'll need to get together the cash to cover them. If you can't save enough money in time, you'll need to review your holiday budget and make cutbacks where you can. Remember: if you pay for anything on your credit card while you're away, you should aim to have enough money sitting in your transaction or savings account at home to cover payment of your credit card balance every month. If not, you'll need to muster all of your strength and discipline to pay it off as soon as you get home (or as soon as you start working again).

4   *How are you going to pay?* Most countries have ATMs that accept Aussie cards. You could also buy a few traveller's cheques before you go as a backup.

Exchange rates, and all that jazz

The value of the Aussie dollar against other currencies will affect you big-time when travelling. If you travel to a country where the Australian dollar is strong you'll be able to buy things more cheaply. Similarly, if you are travelling to a place that has a currency that's strong against the Australian dollar, things will be comparatively expensive. For example, if you travelled to the US in 2001 when the Aussie dollar was valued at around 50 US cents, you would've probably been surviving on a lot of pizza. Flash forward to 2010 when the dollar is sitting sweet above 90 US cents and you might be dining at the top of the Rockefeller Center.

Currency can also play a big role if you're working overseas. For example, you might move to somewhere like the UK with the lure of earning mega-pounds to send home. But what if the pound drops dramatically in value? Currency always fluctuates and circumstances can change quickly so it's always a good idea to err on the side of caution and be conservative with your calculations.

One of the easiest ways to work out how much you're going to get in exchange for your Australian dollars is to jump online. You can convert currency at most banks or at a Bureau de Change, which you'll find at the airport — they'll usually charge you a commission for this.

Currency calculators online

To find an online currency calculator just search for 'currency converter' online—plenty will pop up including the popular <www.xe.com>. There are also currency conversion phone apps that are available to download onto your mobile.

Working overseas

Heading overseas can offer some amazing work and professional development opportunities. If the idea of international work experience floats your boat, you should join the million or so Aussies who are working overseas at any one time.

What comes first, the job or the move?

There are different approaches to working overseas depending on whether you want the security of being set up with a job before you leave Aussie shores, or if you'd prefer to move first and settle into work once you've found your feet. Let's have a look at both:

$ *The job.* If you work for a large multinational organisation it could make it nice and easy to arrange work overseas. Getting a transfer will mean you can hit the ground running and your employer might also help with relocation costs and finding you somewhere to live. If you do score a great offer with a fantastic salary, make sure you do your homework before you sign on the dotted line. Many overseas cities are much more expensive to live in than those in Australia, so your great new wage might not be so great when you take living costs into account. A bit of research will ensure that your expectations are realistic.

$ *The move.* Looking for work when you arrive in a new city means that you'll have time to suss out the scene before you commit to any particular job. That way you'll avoid discovering that you're going to be commuting for an excruciating hour and a half each way every day with your head stuck in someone's armpit. It also means you can meet recruiters face to face and attend interviews in person. The downside is that you won't have cash coming in until you find a job, and who knows how long that will take?

Compare apples with apples

Do your own research to compare the living costs of various cities so you'll be in the best position possible to negotiate your salary if you're moving somewhere expensive. Try searching online for 'Mercer Cost of Living Survey'.

Double whammy

It's bad enough thinking about tax in one country, so brace yourself: if you're living and working OS you'll need to understand your tax obligations in the country you're working in *as well as* in Australia. We know — what a drag. Before you leave, you'll need to determine if you'll still be earning income in Australia (from property or other investments, for example) and therefore if you'll still be considered an Australian resident for tax purposes. While there are no hard and fast rules, your citizenship for tax purposes will generally be based on things such as how your home is used while you're away (if you own your home) and whether you're out of Australia for more than half the year (that is, 183 days). The ATO website has guidelines and case studies to help you: <www.ato.gov.au>. If you have significant investments in Australia, you might be wise to talk to an accountant before you leave — try to find one who's *au fait* with your destination country's tax system as well.

> ## Psst ...
>
> ### For the UK bound: rollover national insurance
>
> If you head to the UK, you'll have to pay national insurance, a tax over-and-above income tax. If you move back to Australia for good at some point, you can roll this over into your Australian super fund — but you have to do this before you leave the UK. You can learn more at First Contact: <www.firstcontact.co.uk>.

Don't forget your super

Each country's superannuation system is different. For example, in neither the US nor the UK is your employer obliged to make super contributions at all.

If your employer is *not* making contributions to your super but you're planning on staying overseas for a good length of time, consider starting up a special savings account into which you transfer money regularly with the goal of investing this money into your super when you get back home. Although it might seem like the last thing you want to do with your money when adventure's around every corner, it really is a great investment in your future and will mean you're not behind the eight ball when you return home. Read more about super in chapter 7.

If your employer *does* make contributions into the equivalent of a superannuation account, consider rolling it over into your Australian super fund when it's time to leave. There's generally a bunch of qualifying criteria you'll need to meet but it's fairly standard practice for Aussies returning home.

Louise's story (age 30)

Doing 'the London thing' was something I'd always wanted to do, so when I turned 27 I decided it was the right time. My initial goals were three-fold: plenty of travel; saving lots of pounds; and trying something new professionally.

Although I'd done a lot of research before I left, I hadn't planned on living in London through Britain's worst recession in 70 years! The latter two goals (saving money and embarking on a new career) have become more difficult. I expected to be in a more positive position financially than if I'd stayed working in Australia for the same period, but this has not turned out to be the case (largely due to unexpected exchange rate fluctuations). On top of that, London is an expensive place to live (apart from the cheap groceries and beer!). On the flipside, I definitely fulfilled my travel goals and have had some amazing experiences and visited some unforgettable places.

Budgeting is more important than ever when moving country. You need to be extra conservative with your estimates of living expenses and the time it might take to get a job. Plus, you never know what might happen after you arrive (the dramatic fall of the British pound, in my case). The constant temptations of weekends away, seeing shows and wining and dining mean it's very easy to burn through your cash—extra vigilance is required!

Louise's story (cont'd)

My advice to other women is to do your homework so you know what to expect. Be sure to research the living costs of the city you're moving to (including market wage rates and likely rent) so your expectations are realistic. Before you head over, make sure that you understand the tax implications of any investments you might have and set up a bank account in your new country beforehand if you can.

Living overseas is a great life experience and, unless you're moving to a tax haven, money will not usually be the primary factor for the move. So enjoy everything a new city, country and culture has to offer—but be smart with your budgeting and planning to make the transition as painless as possible.

Who will look after your stuff?

If you're going overseas for an extended period of time, consider appointing a power of attorney to a friend or relative who can look after your affairs while you're away. The person who has power of attorney over your affairs can act on your behalf to look after your finances and it also gives them access to your private information (so they could deal with your bank on your behalf, if necessary). A power of attorney can be set up through a solicitor or a public trustee in your state or territory. You should also seriously consider writing or updating your will—more about that in chapter 10.

Before you leave on a jet plane

Before you pack your bags, there are a couple of things you should sort out that could make your life much easier when you land at the other end. Here are some tips regarding relocation costs, overseas bank accounts and emergency funds:

§ *Moving and setting up costs.* Be sure to work out what relocating will cost you and aim to have three months worth of living costs saved up, keeping in mind that some cities are more expensive to live in than others and market wage rates vary — we would urge you to be conservative in your budgeting and estimates. It may take you a while to find work and you could be hit up big time for bond and upfront rental costs. If you're looking to rent, two helpful websites are <www.gumtree.co.uk> (UK) and <www.craigslist.com> (US).

§ *Setting up a bank account.* Alas, banking has been a nightmare for many a first-time working holiday maker. Make sure you look into this before you go — it'll make your life a lot easier later on. For example, some banks require a letter from your bank in Australia or require you to have a National Insurance Number (if you're UK bound) or a social security number (if you're heading to the US). Consider using a company like 1st Contact <www.1stcontact.co.uk> if you're heading to the UK — they'll set up a bank account for you for a small fee.

§ *Emergency cash stash.* You never know what's going to happen and when you'll need to get home pronto. *Always* keep a plane flight's worth of cash within reach so you never have to worry about how you'll get home in an emergency.

Investing in you: back to school

We've all been there… the moment during a frustrating day at work when the thought crosses your mind: 'That's it! I've had enough!' More often than not it's just a sign that you need to take a mental health day (and maybe have a few glasses of wine with your girlfriends), but sometimes it's the precursor to something much bigger: a career or life direction change. Heading back to university to study something new might feel like you're taking a big step off a large cliff, but it could end up being one of the most rewarding things you've ever done. After all, it's better to be standing on the low rung of a ladder you want to climb rather than high up on one that you don't.

On the other hand, you might love what you do and be keen to move up the ranks in your profession. Further studying in your area of expertise is a great way to increase your skills and your future earning potential.

Whatever the case may be, there are big financial considerations to take into account — not just course fees, but potential loss of income. Fear not. With careful planning and some temporary sacrifices, you may find yourself better off financially and much happier in the long run.

Working Girl

An oldie but a goodie, *Working Girl* stars Melanie Griffith as Tess McGill ('I have a head for business and a bod for sin'), an ambitious secretary desperate to work her way out of the typing pool and up the corporate ladder. Heaps of fun and very inspirational!

The cost of studying

Make no mistake: going back to university is likely to have a big impact on your finances and therefore on your current lifestyle. Fees are expensive and vary greatly depending on your course and the university you choose. For example, a masters degree could cost anywhere from $20 000 to $60 000 and beyond. Add to that the cost of text books and a computer with good broadband (and don't forget that little thing called your free time).

If you're gasping in horror at the thought of moving back in with your folks, keep in mind that by up-skilling you may well increase not only your knowledge, but also your earning potential. Take the example of MBA course graduates from the Australian Graduate School of Management. A 2008 survey by the *Financial Times* reported that the school's alumni averaged a gob smacking 96 per cent salary increase three years after graduation. Also, think about the joys of having a student card again—cheap public transport and movie tickets, anyone?

You'll need to try to work out exactly what your degree is going to cost you, then budget like there's no tomorrow, working out where you can make any savings (see chapter 2 for tips on budgeting). Yes, you'll probably have to make some sacrifices to your current lifestyle, but remember: it's just for the short term.

Finding the right course — the why, what and how

Finding the right course will take a bit of research, but it's important to take the time to have a good look around in order to track down the perfect course for you.

Psst ...

Try before you buy

Some universities offer shorter programs to help students 'sample' a postgraduate degree, effectively completing it in steps. For example, you could consider starting with a Graduate Certificate (which typically takes one year part-time to complete) then a Graduate Diploma (two years part-time) before moving on to a third year of part-time study to complete a postgraduate Masters degree.

One good way to begin the hunt is to ask yourself the big three questions: why you want to study, what you want to study and where you want to study. Here are our tips:

§   *Why.* The first thing you need to decide is what the purpose of your study is. Is it for personal interest, to develop your career further or to facilitate a change in profession? The answer to these questions will determine how you approach your study and how it can be financed (more about that soon).

§   *What.* You'll then need to select a university and course, taking into account things like the reputation of the school and the curriculum.

§   *Where.* Consider what style of study suits you best. For example, taking an online course means you won't spend any time travelling, but you'll have to exhibit lots of self-discipline. On the other hand, you might prefer face-to-face contact with your lecturer and classmates. Try to make sure you're living in an environment conducive to study — a happy, supportive home life will help you no end.

Open universities

If the thought of being on campus with people 10 years younger freaks you out, check out <www.openuniversities.com.au> where a number of universities have teamed together to offer distance and online courses.

Getting the right balance — part-time versus full-time study

After working out what and where you want to study, your next big decision will be whether to study part time (and perhaps continue working full time) or study full time (and work part time). You'll also need to assess how many subjects you think you can reasonably take on without becoming a stress monkey and weigh that against how quickly you want to complete the degree.

Studying part time means you'll be at it for longer, but you'll still have regular income coming in to help you pay for it. Make sure you ask your employer what sort of study leave support they offer. The other consideration is your time: working full time and studying will be a careful balancing act.

Studying full time means you'll get it over and done with more quickly and allows you to focus and dedicate your time more fully to your study. But it also means that you'll have a loss of income to contend with.

Financing your course — how to pay for it

You'll need to work out where the money is coming from to pay for your course and to keep you afloat if you decide to study full time. Consider the following:

$ *Paying course fees upfront.* If you're studying for an undergraduate degree and pay your full course fees upfront at the start of each semester, you may receive a 20 per cent discount. Similarly, if you make a voluntary repayment of $500 at any stage for either an undergraduate *or* postgraduate degree, you'll receive a 10 per cent discount. This could mean a significant saving over the long term if you can afford it.

$ *Deferring course fees.* The Higher Education Loan Program (HELP) is run by the federal government and offers a suite of interest-free loans to help pay for part or all of your tuition fees. HECS-HELP is HELP's loan facility for undergraduate students and FEE-HELP is for postgraduate students. You'll then have to start repaying the loan through the taxation system once your income reaches a particular threshold. Keep in mind that if you defer your fees you may have to disclose this debt on a home loan application form. For more information, go to <www.goingtouni.gov.au>.

$ *Help from your employer.* If you're taking a course that's in the same field in which you currently work, check in with your employer to find out if they'll help with some or even all of the fees. Make sure you're not doing a deal with the devil, however — some companies will pay for study but only on the grounds that you stay with the company for a certain number of years after you've finished your study.

S   *Help from the government.* If you're studying full time and are 25 years old or over, you may be eligible to receive fortnightly payments through Austudy. Similarly, if you are an indigenous full-time student, you may be able to receive Abstudy. Both depend on your income and assets. Note: if you have income from an investment (such as property) this may affect your eligibility. Check out <www.centrelink.gov.au>.

S   *Applying for a scholarship.* If you're a smartypants, check out any Commonwealth or privately funded scholarships you might be able to apply for. You can find more information from your university or else go to postgraduate scholarship website <www.jason.edu.au>.

S   *Student loan.* If you're not eligible for government support and can't cover your living costs (for example, perhaps you can't work because of your course load) you could look at a student loan — many banks offer these. Make sure you read the conditions of any loan very carefully and fully understand what you're getting into before you sign on the dotted line.

S   *Tax deductions.* Keep in mind that if your course of study is related to the area in which you currently work and your new qualification is likely to help you attain future promotion, your course fees and costs may be tax deductible. Check in with an accountant if you're unsure.

Seeking more information

Universities will have lots of information about their courses, the costs and any financial support you can apply for (they want your business after all!). Search online or give them a call. Consider attending information nights to talk over your options in person. Finally, talk to other people you know who've gone back to study — they often have good advice having been there themselves.

Family matters: up the duff

If you've decided to turn two into three, brace yourself: that little bundle of joy is going to turn into a money-muncher. Babies are expensive — as in, cost-of-a-house expensive.

According to a 2007 *AMP NATSEM Income Wealth Report*, the average cost of raising two children from birth to the age of 21 in Australia was $537 000. In 2009 another social researcher put the 'real' cost of raising a child who lives at home until they're 24 (including private tutoring, sports and dance classes and so on) at just over a million dollars.

Before you go reaching for the Ansell packet, it's reassuring to know that costs start off small when your child is young and then increase as the years go on. The good thing about that is that you have time to plan and prepare. Rest assured that most parents seem to universally agree that their children are the best investment they ever made!

Pre-bubby

Even before your partner starts to get that amorous twinkle in their eye, there are important things to consider when you're planning a family, including whether you want to go public or private, what sort of baby stuff you'll need to buy and what parental leave entitlements you can receive. We'll take you through some of them now.

Health insurance

When you have a baby you can choose to give birth to your little bambino through the public system or else through the private system by taking out private health insurance. Whether to go public or private is a fairly contentious topic amongst mothers. The approach that's right for you really comes down to where you live, what sort of hospitals are available to you and personal choice. If you decide to have a baby through the public system, your prenatal visits and the birth should be covered by Medicare — but check out <www.medicare.gov.au> to be sure that this is the case in your area and for your current situation. If you want your own midwife to help guide you through pregnancy and act as your support during labour, expect to pay around a few thousand dollars. If you'd prefer to go private (which gives you options such as choosing your own doctor) you'll need to take out private health insurance *before* you become pregnant. Note that private health insurance may not pay for all of your costs and you'll more than likely foot some of the bill. You'll have to check this out carefully with different health insurers.

Buying baby stuff

You'll need to start buying stuff for your bubby — there's a whole brave new baby world out there. Think: cot, car seat, pram, nappies upon nappies and more. If you're doing it on the cheap, start with hand-me-downs from friends. Because babies grow so quickly, second-hand clothes can be almost brand-spanking new. For equipment, consider buying factory seconds or end-of-line products and samples and don't forget good old eBay. Alternatively, take full advantage of your family's joy at your little addition and gratefully accept any generous offers they might make! They'll feel good contributing and it'll save you a little bit of stress.

Parental leave entitlements

One of the first things you'll need to do when you're planning a family is to check out your work entitlements. Some things to consider are:

§ *Federal government regulations.* According to the National Employment Standards, a permanent employee (man or woman) who has worked for 12 months of continuous service is generally entitled to up to 12 months unpaid parental leave and can then request a further 12 months of unpaid leave, which can only be refused on 'reasonable business grounds.' From 2011, paid parental leave is due to kick in. Visit <www.familyassist.gov.au> for more information.

$ *Your employer's policy.* Employers must stick to government regulations but in addition to this will also have their own policies, which can vary widely between sectors and employers. Leave is generally unpaid unless your contract or company policy states otherwise, and some industries are more generous than others. For example, government, finance and insurance industries are more likely to offer paid parental leave while industries such as retail and hospitality are far less likely. Make sure you keep this in mind before signing a contract with a new employer.

Be sure to talk to your employer about your entitlements, company policy and whether any sort of flexible arrangements apply. For example, if you're entitled to paid leave, find out if you could you take some weeks on full pay and some weeks on part pay if that would suit you best. Or would they negotiate on flexible work arrangements when you return to work?

Post-bubby

It's a whole new financial world out there post 'mini me', and as a woman you face having to take more into consideration than a man when deciding to have a baby. Right at the top of the list is understanding what taking time off work to raise your little tacker will do to your finances — both in the immediate and not-so-immediate future.

The impact of taking time off work

Taking time off work after having a baby will have an enormous impact on your life. According to the Australian Institute of Families Studies, the average loss of income by the primary carer to raise a child is estimated to be $160 000.

You'll need to talk to your partner about your game plan. Do you want to be the primary carer for the first few years of your child's life, or do you want (or need) to return to paid work? And if so, do you have family close by to help out with babysitting or will your baby be put into child care? Costs for childcare vary widely, but at the last census in 2006 it averaged $215 a week. You'll need to redo your budget to take into account all these new changes and revise your financial goals accordingly. Remember that with a baby around you probably won't be going out as much, so you may actually spend less than you used to.

If you do stay at home and become the primary caregiver, it's vital that you're equally involved in all financial decisions. Just because you're not bringing home the bacon doesn't mean you're not making a contribution, that your contribution isn't equal, or that your right to use your joint income is any less. From all accounts, staying at home to look after a baby or child is one of the hardest and most time-consuming jobs you could ever take on! You can read more about how to negotiate the tricky side of love and money in chapter 11.

Don't forget that every year you're not in the paid workforce, there's no income going into your superannuation from your employer. One of the disadvantages of taking time out of the workforce to become the primary caregiver (particularly the case for women) is that you're likely to ultimately end up with much less in your super account than your partner. As such you should talk to him or her about making a regular contribution out of the household income into your super. Read more about the importance of super in chapter 7.

Doing it for your country

The Australian Government offers a wide range of financial assistance to help raise children, from the baby bonus (around $5000 per child paid in instalments) to family tax and childcare benefits. What you're eligible for depends on things like household income and the number and age of any children you have.

After you've given birth in hospital, you'll get a government assistance information pack and forms to take home. If you'd like to be a bit more organised than that, you can get information at Medicare and Centrelink offices or online at <www.familyassist.gov.au>.

Penny-pinching parents

According to a 2006 survey by Bankwest, more than a quarter of parents have pinched or been tempted to pinch money from their children's savings. While the number one reason was to purchase everyday essentials, 16 per cent said it was to afford extravagances such as a holiday or new car!

Doing it for the kids

A 2006 survey by the Commonwealth Bank found that 47 per cent of parents do not feel financially prepared to meet the cost of educating their children. By starting saving early on you have time and our favourite friend — compound interest — on your side to give your child a head start. Consider putting your baby bonus into a managed fund (see chapter 6) or setting up an education fund if you're thinking about private education where fees can be gob-smackingly high. You would be well-advised to see an accountant to help you with this.

A word of warning: beware the tax man! While it might be tempting to put an investment in your child's name, you should seek professional advice before doing anything along these lines. Tax can be a killer as there is a special tax on the unearned income of minors. Visit <www.ato.gov.au> for more information.

> ### Great baby books
>
> If you want to prepare yourself for bubsville, check out *Up the Duff* by Kaz Cooke (Penguin, 2009). A hugely entertaining look at everything you'll need to know about pregnancy and preparing for a bubby. For a closer look at the financial side of things, try *How to Afford a Baby: The Nine Month Plan to Finance Having a Child* by Justine Davies (ABC Books, 2007).

Windfalls: inheritance and the lottery

So now we come to the fun part of the book. The bit where you get to dream about having that fortune fall unexpectedly into your lap one day without having to do a snippet of hard work. But alas, even inheritances and lottery wins come with their own set of problems and cautionary tales. Read on to learn that the reality doesn't always live up to the dream ...

Inheriting a fortune

The chances are that most of us probably *won't* inherit a fortune, but you may well inherit something at some point in your life. While it would be somewhat ideal if it came from a rich, reclusive relative you didn't know, unfortunately it's most likely to come from someone close — your parents or a partner later on in life.

While coming into a large sum of money might provide financial relief, it can also cause problems. The issues range from the heavy stuff — making us think about what comes next (The Big Guy in the Sky and all that) to coming to grips with how to invest it wisely and dealing with family members who may not necessarily have the same ideas or goals as you. (They may not agree with what you'd like to do with Nanna's old house, for example.)

There are a few guiding rules when it comes to dealing with an inheritance:

§   *Take your time.* There shouldn't be any reason to do anything quickly. Decisions are never good when they're emotional, particularly financial ones!

§   *Consider all your options.* Think about your goals and how your inheritance could help you to reach them. Don't feel guilty; think of your inheritance as a gift that could really make a difference to your future.

§   *Seek the advice of a professional.* When you're ready, seek the help of a financial adviser or an accountant. There's a lot to consider and professional advice is definitely the way to go.

Winning the lottery

It's the moment we all dream of: you happen to stop by the newsagent on the way home from work and buy yourself a ticket to the Tattslotto draw that night. Later that evening, you're on the couch, wine in hand, watching the fifth TV re-run of *Love Actually*, and then it happens ... *your* numbers flash up on screen and in an instant your whole life changes. You live the rest of your life without a care in the world, happily ever after ...

Okay — reality time. Your chances of winning the lottery are pretty slim, to say the least. To be more exact, they are one in eight million (to win Tattslotto), one in 45 million (to win Super7 OzLotto) and one in 54 million (to win Powerball). Statistically speaking, you're much more likely to be struck by lightning (one in 1.6 million), give birth to twins (one in 44 — yikes!) or even be seen at an André Rieu concert (*yikes!!*).

The other thing about coming into a sudden windfall is that it doesn't necessarily bring everlasting happiness. Every year we see another story on *Today Tonight* about a lottery winner who's now lost everything or who fell out with their family or who went crazy from all the attention and now lives in a cave. In fact, a widely cited 1999 study by the Certified Financial Planning Standards Board in the US estimated one third of lottery winners ended up going bankrupt. Even more startling is a National Endowment for Financial Education study which reported that up to 70 per cent of people who receive large lump sums of money blow it in a few years.

So, given all this, rather than spending $10 on a weekly lottery ticket, we have a couple of other ideas for you:

$ If you put the $10 that you would have spent on a lottery ticket every week into a savings account instead (in this example earning 5 per cent interest per annum) and didn't touch it for the next 30 years you'd have somewhere near $35 000 at the end.

$ If you put that $10 each week into an aggressive growth superannuation fund and it earned on average 11.5 per cent per annum (the rate that ASIC say is reasonable to expect this type of fund to return over the long term), 30 years later you'd have somewhere in the vicinity of $120 000.

We know what we'd prefer to do.

part IV
the secret
to financial
success

Well, you've made it to the end of your money makeover ... or have you? There's still something really important you need to know. In fact, it could mean the difference between achieving your goals (and becoming a financial guru) or just having a lot of good intentions.

When we started writing this book we wanted to know what it was that set really high financial achievers apart from the also-rans. We knew it wasn't how much they earned or how high their IQ might be. So if this wasn't the case, what the hell was it?!

After many nights of contemplation over a wine (or two) and lots of research we think, by Jove, we've got it. So without further ado ... the secret to financial success!

the secret revealed

There once was a girl called Bree
Whose marks were the worst in grade three
A determined young thing
She knuckled down with a grin
And years later she topped her degree.

First things first. If you've skipped here to learn the secret to financial success before reading everything else, go back to where you came from quick smart!

As we mentioned way back in our introduction, women have all the right tools for being great investors — better investors than men. We act with less bravado than men, we're more likely to research and to seek advice than men and we're less likely to jump from investment to investment in the hope of making a quick (and big) buck than men. So you've already got it all over them.

But there's something you need to know about what it is that sets the really great investors apart from the crowd — the secret to financial success. And once you know that, there'll be no stopping you. We're now going to talk about what it is that's going to make you a *really* successful investor — and potentially very wealthy too. In this chapter we'll cover:

ⓢ   why some people are successful financially and others are not: the secret revealed

ⓢ   making the secret work for you: tips to help you write up your own plan

ⓢ   how the secret works in practise: an example of a plan

ⓢ   sticking to your plan: how to stay motivated.

Why some people are successful financially and others are not: the secret revealed

Do you ever wonder why some people seem to have that Midas touch while others struggle with money all their lives? Do you ever look at people who have money and wonder how they did it, what their secret is?

All is not what it would seem

It might appear that some people have had a lucky ride. While that might be so in some cases, it's much more likely that there's more going on behind the scenes than meets the eye.

Back in the 1970s two researchers by the names of Thomas Stanley and William Danko set out to find out exactly what it was that made people wealthy. They wanted to know what set rich people apart from those who'd never 'made it'. They spent two decades interviewing thousands of Americans (those who were rich and those who were not) and what they discovered blew all of their previous ideas out of the water. They discovered that wealth is not accumulated by earning a large income, and it's very rarely about luck (winning or inheriting money). It's not even about intelligence. Wealth is, in fact, more often the result of a lifestyle of hard work, self-discipline, perseverance and planning.

What's the good news about Stanley and Danko's findings? It confirms that wealth isn't only available to a lucky few. It means that you can achieve it, too.

Plan to be wealthy

Studies have shown time and time again that you'll give yourself the best chance of reaching your financial goals if you plan. According to a study sponsored by the Consumer Federation of America and NationsBank Corporation, consumers who develop financial plans nearly double the amount they save compared with those who do not. Financial investment literature has backed this up with research indicating that households who had not written up a financial plan had accumulated significantly less wealth than households that had. Stanley and Danko also conclude that from their own studies there's a strong correlation between planning and wealth accumulation.

In other words, people who make the effort to create a financial plan — who write down their goals as well as exactly what they're going to do in order to reach them — are giving themselves the best chance possible to realise their financial dreams. You might have heard the old adage 'you can't hit a target you can't see'. Well, that's what we're talking about here — and it's the secret to financial success.

Making the secret work for you: tips to help you write up your own plan

When you're writing your plan, the key is to decide on your goals and then to spell them out clearly, ensuring that they are measurable. Clear and specific goals provide a yardstick by which you can measure your achievements. It's not enough to say 'I want to be rich someday'; it'll only work if you're *specific* about exactly what you want to achieve.

Go back and revisit the short-term, medium-term, long-term and super-long-term goals you wrote down while you were reading chapter 1. Ensure that they are clear and specific. For example, for a short-term goal, instead of: 'Take an overseas holiday', it would be much better to write: 'Save $8000 to travel throughout South America for three months in two years' time'. This makes your goal specific and will make it much easier for you to work out exactly how you're going to obtain it.

The next part of the process is to write down whatever action you plan to take in order to reach your goals — perhaps something you plan to do every week or month to contribute towards each goal. Your actions should be very specific. It's also important to make sure that your planned actions are realistic and attainable. If you discover that your goals are going to be virtually impossible to achieve (for example, perhaps you'd over-enthusiastically planned to save 75 per cent of your take-home-pay every week) you run the risk of thinking it's all too hard and giving up. Obviously, this should be avoided at all costs! So make sure you take your income into account when you're working out how you're going to achieve your goals. You should already know roughly how much you can save each week or month based on the budget you set up earlier and this should enable you to have a good stab at working out how much and how quickly you'll be able to save.

To give you an example, if one of your goals is to invest in a property in five years how might you work out how you're going to reach it? Take a look at this example.

Example: Imaginary Ingrid's goal

→ *Goal:* save enough to buy my own apartment worth $400000 in five years.

→ *Action:* in order to reach my goal I must save $100000 ($80000 to pay for the deposit, approximately $17500 to pay for stamp duty (the apartment will be purchased in Victoria) and approximately $2500 to cover other buying costs). To do this I'm going to set up an online savings account immediately and arrange to have $340 automatically transferred from my everyday transaction account into my online savings account once a week.

Keep in mind that Ingrid's annual income is $55 000 and she brings home an $850 pay cheque every week. She spends $180 on rent per week and approximately $210 on other living expenses, leaving her with $460 to play with. So saving $340 per week is realistic. We don't want to suggest it's going to be easy — five years of constant saving towards a deposit for an apartment is going to take a lot of dedication and perseverance. But just think what satisfaction it'll bring when she picks up the keys to her new apartment!

Make sense? By breaking your goal down in this way, it immediately becomes clear exactly what you have to do to reach your goal — and that'll get you on track straight away.

In a nutshell, the three steps you'll need to take in order to reach your financial goals are:

1   Decide on your goals.

2   Write down your goals (making them clear, measurable and attainable).

3   Write down the action/s you're going to take to meet each goal (making each action very specific).

Reviewing your plan

Once you've written down your plan and you're working your way towards reaching your goals, you should review your plan on a regular basis. It's important to keep an eye on your goals, and how you're tracking against them, by referring back to them now and then. We suggest you keep a list of your goals close by, perhaps in the folder you keep your banking statements in, or in your diary.

It's quite likely that your long-term and super-long-term goals will change over time. For example, you might think twice about that early retirement to the Maldives and start working towards some other goal instead. This might mean that your plan changes over time. That's okay. The main thing is that you're working towards providing for your future.

Seeking help to set up your plan

If you feel you need help writing up your goals into a comprehensive financial plan it would be well worth your money to seek the advice of a licensed financial adviser. This is their speciality — they'll help you to establish your financial goals and set up a plan to work towards them. If you don't have a financial adviser already we tell you where you can find one in the 'Help when you need it' section at the back of this book.

How the secret works in practise: an example of a plan

Writing up your own simple financial plan (where you list your goals and the action you're committing to take to achieve each one) doesn't have to be difficult. In fact, it gives you a chance to get creative as you work out exactly what you want and devise a way to get it. Here's an example.

Fabricated Fiona is a 30-year-old kindergarten teacher who had never been particularly interested in money or investing — until a year ago when a conversation with a friend inspired her to do something about her finances. Fiona read a book or two and developed a plan to start saving towards her goals. Luckily, she didn't have any credit card debt so her first task was to save up an 'emergency fund' to cover her living expenses for six months. Now that's done she's decided on three goals she'd like to start working towards.

There are a few things that Fiona will need to take into account when writing her plan to ensure that it will work in practice. One of the most important is to work out a realistic amount to save after living expenses have been deducted from her salary. Fiona earns an annual salary of $48 000 and brings home a weekly wage of approximately $750. After working out her budget early in the year, she's expecting to spend around $180 per week on living expenses as well as $200 a week on rent. With these factors in mind, Fiona writes up her plan.

Example: Fabricated Fiona's plan

Here's an example of a simple plan Fiona might write down to help her reach her three goals.

→ *Goal 1:* save $10 000 for a two-month European vacation in two years.

 Action: in order to reach my goal I will immediately open an online savings account and have $95 automatically transferred from my everyday transaction account into this account every week.

→ *Goal 2:* buy $50 000 worth of Australian blue chip shares over five years.

 Action: in order to reach my goal I'll immediately open a second online savings account and have $170 automatically transferred to this account from my everyday transaction account every week. Whenever the balance of my savings account hits $5000 I'll withdraw the money and buy a parcel of Australian blue chip shares (with a focus on companies that pay franked dividends) until I've invested a total of $50 000.

→ *Goal 3:* save enough to retire at the age of 65 with an annual income of $39 000 (in today's dollars).

 Action: in order to reach my goal I will immediately start salary sacrificing $50 per week into my employer's super fund (the growth fund option). I will also contribute $1000 in after-tax dollars to my superannuation fund every year in order to qualify for the government co-contribution.

Fiona can calculate how much she's going to need to save to reach each of her goals using the savings and superannuation calculators on most banking websites (or by using the calculators at <www.fido.gov.au>).

It's quite likely that Fiona's goals will change over time as her circumstances change: perhaps she will get a pay increase and decide she can afford to be saving more or she might opt to save for a house deposit rather than a share portfolio. Don't forget that inflation will take its toll on her savings over time, particularly on her long-term and super-long-term funds, such as superannuation. So Fiona's goal of working towards retiring on an annual income of $39 000 (in today's dollars) will need to be increased over time to account for this.

Whatever happens, Fiona should adjust her goals and actions accordingly. The important thing is that she gets started as soon as possible. Fiona's particularly lucky in that she's got time on her side, but remember that you're never too old to set up a plan for yourself. If you are older, or if you feel you'd like the help of a professional to help you write up a comprehensive financial plan, it'd be a very good idea to see a licensed financial adviser. That's the kind of thing they do for a living!

Sticking to your plan: how to stay motivated

Whenever we catch a glimpse of the world's high achievers in action, it's easy to put them up on a pedestal and wish we'd been lucky enough to have scored the talent genes. We watch the Olympics every few years and most of us imagine how wonderful it would be to be an athlete competing at such an elite level and how amazing it would feel to win a gold medal. We envy the Nobel Prize winner who's discovered the cure for a disease set to alleviate the misery of people around the globe. Plenty of people would probably give just about anything to be able to make such a contribution.

What you shouldn't forget is that Olympians and Nobel Prize winners are people who've been working towards their goal for many, many years. That's the bit we don't see — the dedication and the endless days and nights of hard work it's taken to get there.

While we certainly wouldn't want to suggest that sticking to a plan to reach your financial goals is as difficult as setting out to win an Olympic gold, we won't pretend it's going to be easy. Keeping your goals at the forefront of your mind over many years and paying attention to the little things that will help you reach them — day in, day out — can be hard work. For one thing, you're likely to find your path twisting and turning as your circumstances change. For example, if you're single now and planning for your future, things will probably change if you meet the person of your dreams and your 'I' becomes a 'we.' That's just natural.

The important thing is to keep a vision in mind of where you want to end up; how you get there might change, but if you want something badly enough now, the chances are that your end-goal is going to stay the same over time, no matter what might happen in the shorter term.

The carrot on the stick

While you might not have the lure of a gold medal or a Nobel Prize spurring you on, the dream of a prosperous future that enables you to live the life you really want should be a strong motivator. The question is, how do you stay focused if things start to get tough, or if you become consumed by day-to-day living and you forget about that goal you set that you won't realise for many years to come? There are a number of things you can do to help yourself — here are some suggestions.

Keep your plan visible

As we've already discussed, writing down your plan is a very important part of the process. Keeping your notes somewhere visible is one way to keep your plan top of mind — perhaps stick your notes to the fridge or keep them in a prominent spot on your desk. You could write down your plan on the first page of your new diary every year. This is a really good way of making a yearly review of your plan a habit and makes it more likely that you'll regularly assess your progress and make changes if necessary.

Tell someone else about your plan

Sharing your plan with a friend or family member might make you feel vulnerable, but it will also make you more accountable when your friend asks you how you're going! Better still, encourage someone else to start along the path to financial freedom too. Just like having a running buddy, it can be really helpful to have someone working alongside you who understands what you're doing and who's there to give you encouragement when you need it.

Form an investment group

Just like a book group, regularly getting together with a group of like-minded friends to discuss finance-related topics can be a great way of learning and discussing your financial goals (and how you're tracking towards reaching them) and can be an excellent way of staying motivated. However you decide to do it, stay focused and always keep your end goal in mind!

The nitty-gritty

Make sure you keep any paperwork (or emails) that come through from your bank or other financial institutions and always check them to make sure that everything is A-Okay. If you really get into it, you could set up a spreadsheet on which you chart all of your investments, noting down whenever the balance changes, when you've contributed extra funds, if interest or dividends have been paid or if your share price rises or falls. This will allow you to see at a glance how you're tracking against your targets.

Keep on moving forward

There might be times when you feel like you're going backwards. For example, you have money invested in shares but the share market takes a temporary dive (and so does your portfolio balance, if only on paper). Or, you have to withdraw money from your online savings account because an unexpected expense rears its ugly head.

Whatever you do, don't get discouraged. In order to keep moving towards your targets you'll just have a bit of extra work to do. For example, it might be a case of looking back over your budget and working out if there's any way you can save any extra money. If reaching your goals is that important to you, you'll have to prioritise them and make sacrifices in some other area in order to stay on track. For example, you might have been saving for a European holiday in two years but have just had to fork out for some expensive repairs on your car and your savings account has done a bit of a nose dive. You'll just have to forgo some other expense in order to get there. You get the idea.

It's up to you!

So there it is, the secret to financial success: forming a workable plan to reach your goals and then committing to sticking to it over time until you get there. It's not rocket science; in fact, the most remarkable thing about it is its simplicity. But the great thing about it is that it works and it's available to just about anyone who wants to make their financial dreams a reality. It's up to you!

Final thoughts

So here you are at the end of your money makeover. You've survived the murky depths of managed funds and superannuation, learnt how to deal with your partner's dodgy money habits and you now know the secret to making it all happen. Now it's time to take action — it's not enough to just know all this stuff and be able to reel it off to impress the accountant sitting beside you at your next dinner party. You need to commit to doing something about it.

It's easy to feel paralysed with information overload, or to freeze with uncertainty not knowing if you're about to make the right financial decision. The thing is, there is no right or wrong. As long as you've done your research, there are many paths you could take. Remember, you can always start small. Once you take the plunge, you'll be amazed at how good you feel when your savings and investments start to grow and you can see that reaching your goals is, in fact, a possibility. You just have to be brave.

We sincerely hope you've found this book both useful and enjoyable. We'd be extremely chuffed if in 30 years time, as you're sitting on your yacht in Majorca or signing over a hefty cheque to charity, your thoughts flickered back to that blue money make-over book you picked up one day in a bookstore, which set you on your path to financial success.

We wish you every happiness and a brilliant financial future.

help when you need it

There'll be times throughout your life as an investor when you're likely to find that you need the help of a professional or two. Where should you start your search?

Accountant

Find a chartered accountant at <www.charteredaccountants.com.au> or a certified practising accountant at <www.cpaaustralia.com.au>.

Financial adviser

To find a licensed financial adviser go to the Financial Planning Association of Australia's website <www.fpa.asn.au>. If you're after a financial adviser who specialises in responsible investment products, have a look at the Responsible Investment Association Australasia website <www.responsibleinvestment.org>.

ASIC's consumer website FIDO <www.fido.gov.au> has lots of great tips about what to look for when you're choosing a financial adviser and it's definitely worth checking this out before you see anyone.

You'll often pay a one-off fee for advice from a financial adviser, but be aware that most of them will also receive commissions or bonuses from the financial institutions whose products they recommend and invest your money in. For this reason we recommend you find a financial adviser who's happy to charge you for their time, rather than being paid on a commission basis. That way you can be more confident you're receiving unbiased advice.

Insurance broker

If you're on the hunt for insurance (particularly one of the trickier, more complicated kinds such as life insurance) you'll probably find it useful to speak to an insurance broker. You can search for one on the National Insurance Brokers Association of Australia website <www.niba.com.au>.

Solicitor

Search for a qualified solicitor via the Law Institute or Law Society in your state or territory.

$ Law Institute of Victoria: <www.liv.asn.au>

$ Law Society of the ACT: <www.actlawsociety.com.au>

$ Law Society of New South Wales: <www.lawsociety.com.au>

$ Law Society Northern Territory: <www.lawsocietynt.asn.au>

$ Law Society of South Australia: <www.lawsocietysa.asn.au>

$ Law Society of Tasmania: <www.taslawsociety.asn.au>

$ Law Society of WA: <www.lawsocietywa.asn.au>

$ Queensland Law Society: <www.qls.com.au>.

Stockbroker

The Australian Securities Exchange (ASX) offers a 'find a broker' service which is very useful <www.asx.com.au>. ASIC's consumer website, FIDO <www.fido.gov.au> also has a list of questions to ask your potential broker to make sure you get the right one for you.

For other information on all things financial...

If you're looking for general financial information try these helpful websites for starters.

Australian Securities and Investments Commission

ASIC's consumer website, FIDO, is a great resource for all things financial — lots of tips on budgeting, saving and investing, how to cope with debt and with great investment calculators you can use: <www.fido.gov.au>.

Australian Taxation Office

This might be one you'd been hoping to get through life avoiding, however the ATO's website is very helpful if you need information about anything tax-related: <www.ato.gov.au>.

Moneygirl

For one-click links to all of the websites mentioned in this book and lots of other information to boot (including weekly forums) check out <www.moneygirl.com.au>.

index

Index